AMBUSHED!

THE SIREN SONG OF ALCOHOL USE

THE SIREN SONG OF
ALCOHOL USE

AMBUSHED!

DR. GUY E. GLAD
PHD, DSL

CONTENTS

ABBREVIATIONS

AA   Alcoholics Anonymous

APA   American Psychiatric Association

ASAM   American Society of Addiction Medicine

AUD   Alcohol-Use Disorder

CR   Celebrate Recovery

DSM-5   Diagnostic and Statistical Manual of Mental Disorders, 5th Edition

GNC   God's New Covenant: A New Testament Translation

HCSB   Holman Christian Standard Bible

NA   Narcotics Anonymous

NASB   New American Standard Bible

NIV   New International Version of the Bible

NLT   New Living Translation of the Bible

TEV   Today's English Version

PREFACE TO THE SECOND PRINTING

Since the first printing of this book, our family suffered a tragic, alcohol-related loss of a beloved family member. This family member was a committed Christian, gifted musician, husband, and father. He regularly ministered musically throughout the Rocky Mountain region of the United States. Along with his talented and gifted wife they would provide the highest quality praise and worship music, not only at churches but also at special events. His God-given musical abilities were a constant reminder of the grace and blessings God had bestowed upon him.

However, he developed an escalating use of alcohol that evolved to abuse over time, leading to his tragic and painful death. He left behind a grieving widow and emotionally wounded eight-year-old daughter, both also blessed and gifted by God with their own unique talents and skills. As I write this both of them continue to grieve the traumatic loss of their husband and father.

As I witnessed this family member's physical, emotional, and spiritual decline over time due to alcohol abuse, two thoughts echoed in my mind, First, *this tragedy did not have to happen.* Second, and ironically so, *both the Bible and this book remained on a shelf in his home, acknowledged but unread by him.* The alcohol abuse had grown into the monster of dependence. To this day the entire family continues to mourn his untimely and unnecessary passing.

This experience confirmed for me the need for this second printing of *Ambushed! The Siren Song of Alcohol Use.* It is my hope and prayer for this printing to reach even more people who are in a search for forgiveness, grace, and freedom from the ravages of alcohol abuse. God's grace is not only sufficient but transcendent over the specter of alcohol misuse. May God bless you richly as you read this book for yourself and for use with others for whom you care.

-Dr. Guy E. Glad, PhD, DSL

September 2024

ACKNOWLEDGMENTS

As I began to write this book, I realized there exists an overwhelming number of individuals for whom I am eternally thankful, all of whom I desire to acknowledge and publicly show my appreciation. However, the reality of space limitations will not allow full expression of a grateful heart.

First, I want to acknowledge and thank four specific individuals who have served as mentors to me; Drs. Ronald Boehme, Jay Diller, James Gibson, and James Tille. Each one of you have, for some reason unknown to me, consistently shown me encouragement, patience, guidance, and friendship. You have become beacons of light and guides over challenging life terrain. Your "example to all" attitude (see First Timothy 3:12), embedded in your hearts, has provided inspiration to me to pass on to others what I have seen and learned from you. Thank you.

Next, I want to thank my father. Due to your alcohol misuse and consistent verbal abuse of me and my beloved mother, I remember feeling only three emotions toward you growing up; anger, disgust, and embarrassment. However, thanks to God's unending patience and renewing grace, you accepted Christ a short time before your death, resulting in genuine change. While I was not there physically to witness this, my best friend at the time informed me that after praying to receive Christ, you cried like a baby. Your repentance and forgiveness were real. God transformed you from an abusive, angry, racist, drunk, to a man of calmness, peace, and sobriety. Dad, your life taught me these two things: that alcohol misuse ruins lives and relationships, but the grace of God, active within the spiritual maturity process, can change it all. Thank you for these twin life lessons. My feelings for you have since transformed into fondness, understanding, and thankfulness for God's grace in your life and mine.

I also want to broadcast to the world my grateful and thankful heart for my lovely wife Donna. Your patience, perseverance, encouragement, and love toward me is a daily presence in my life. Without your gracious attitude and desire to stand by my side through a challenging and demanding time of life, I would not have been able to complete this book. You have infused calmness and peace into the midst of a whirlwind of activity. Thank you and I love you.

Finally, and most importantly, I want to thank my Lord and Savior Jesus Christ. There are not enough adjectives in the English language to sufficiently express the depth of gratitude and love my heart feels for You. The partnering work of the Trinity in my life has been palpable. The protection, preparation, and calling of God the Father; the atoning, cleansing, forgiving, and transforming work of Christ through the cross and His physical resurrection from the dead; and the convicting, teaching, and guiding work of the Holy Spirit, have been pivotal and conspicuous throughout my life since the point of my salvation as a high school senior.

Without Your love, encouragement, and personal ownership You have branded on my heart and soul, I would be capable of nothing. You have motivated me to bring You into all areas of my life, including this book. Thank You, Lord. I love You and owe You all that I am, as well as my eternal destiny in Your presence. Despite the pain and disappointment of my personal sins and failures, my enduring goal in life is to do all for Your glory. To You belongs the glory and praise forever.

"So whether you eat or drink, or whatever you do, do it all for the glory of God."

First Corinthians 10:31

WHY I WROTE THIS BOOK

Distraction. This is the bane of spiritual growth for Christians. Especially in contemporary America. Finances, careers, material possessions, relationships, and emotionalism (especially those activities that trigger the reward center of the brain resulting in "feeling good"), are some issues that raise anxiety and elicit such questions:

- Where will I live?

- What will be my career?

- How will I pay the bills?

- Who will I marry?

- How can I deal with my negative emotions like disappointment, fear, failure, abandonment, loneliness, and just plain feeling bad?

- If alcohol can help me feel good again, or at least help me to temporarily forget my pain, then what is the harm?

- What do I need to do to feel good again?

These questions, and many others, have the potential to create uphill challenges and seemingly insurmountable problems for Christians. The final question in the above list of queries is especially applicable for contemporary Christians. I have personal knowledge of these questions and dynamics, having experienced all of these questions, especially the questions about dealing with negative emotions and finally feeling good again.

In his historically classic work reflecting major themes in Greek mythology, Homer's *Odyssey* presents the reader with a recurring theme and intermittent personalities sprinkled throughout Greek writings and mythology, like the Sirens and their alluring songs. Living on an Aegean island, these creatures were half human, half beast, and would lure non-vigilant sailors to their destruction. The seductive songs of the Sirens were virtually irresistible, and sounded like smooth honey, promising joy, fulfillment, and knowledge, but in the end delivering destruction and death. The following summary succinctly summarizes this deadly danger:

Homer wrote of Odysseus and the Sirens, whose beautiful song lured countless sailors to shipwreck on the rocky island of Anthemoessa. Odysseus knew that he must pass the Sirens before he would be reunited with his homeland, so he took action to protect the lives of his sailors and himself. Odysseus plugged all of his sailors' ears with beeswax and ordered them to tie him to the mast. The Sirens would beg the sailors to let him go, but he gave strict orders: No matter what he said, the sailors, under no circumstances, could untie his binds. Odysseus understood that his personality would change when he was subjected to temptation. That his willpower would wane. That, without some sort of preventative device, he would lose all control and give in to temptation. The ship drifted toward the feared chasm. The sailors patiently waited. Without notice, the sailors recognized a sudden calm. They ensured their ears were plugged and tied Odysseus to the mast—just as they came within earshot of the island. "'Come here," the Sirens sang, "renowned Odysseus, honor to the Achaean name, and listen to our two voices. No one ever sailed past us without staying to hear the enchanting sweetness of our song, and he who listens will go on his way not only charmed, but wiser, for we know all the ills that the gods laid upon the Argives and Trojans before Troy, and can tell you everything that is going to happen over the whole world." This was the enchanting song of temptation, that which had caused many a sailor to perish. But Odysseus had used a technique that Daniel Akst calls *precommitment*—one of the most effective devices for behavioral and habit change. For as Odysseus knew that his willpower would fail as he approached temptation, he also knew that capitulation would mean his demise. Instead, he decided to take action to protect his future self from, well, himself by *creating a system that made failure impossible.* The song of the Sirens isn't any more tempting than the call of the buzzing phone, or the dinging email notification, or the delicious Coca-Cola. And the few times that we, as modern citizens, try to protect ourselves from indulging, we say something like, "I shouldn't eat that, so I won't eat it anymore." And then, when we find ourselves approaching the temptation, we buckle and yield and find ourselves only strengthening the neural path of a bad habit. How many times have you heard your friend painfully say, "I'm never drinking again" only to find him wobbling home from the bar the next day? Odysseus, however, knew that there is a way to protect against one's temporally separated future self. He precommited to an action, while in his sane state, in a manner that was impossible to cancel. Even though his future self would want to escape, he made compliance absolutely obligatory.[1] (emphasis mine).

If you have any alcohol-related experiences similar to what Odysseus faced with the mythological Siren song, then this book is for you. Regarding your alcohol use, have you ever isolated yourself, kept secrets, lied to friends and family members, lost a job, faced financial crisis, encountered broken relationships, or traversed humiliating legal problems? If you answered "yes" to any of these questions, then read on.

Two concepts taken from Odysseus' experience with the Siren songs apply to the Christian life: alcohol misuse presents an alluring song that, in the end, results in destruction, and a precommitment to neutralize this devastation is required. For the Christian, a proper understanding of biblical principles of alcohol use in combination with medical research,

---

1   "Odysseus, Precommitment, and the Siren Song," Hack the System, last modified October 2, 2012, accessed June 2, 2019, http://hackthesystem.com/ blog/ odysseus-precommitment-and-the-siren-song/.

provides an invaluable foundation to living the successful Christian life, even in the face of sometimes overwhelming temptation. And Homer's concept of precommitment is a clear reminder of the Christian response to the daily climate of "persistent temptation" we all face.

"Trust in the LORD with all your heart; do not depend on your own understanding. Seek his will in all you do, and he will show you which path to take" (Proverbs 3:5-6). This biblical principle of precommitment applies to all situations in life, including decisions regarding alcohol use.

I am an adult child of an alcoholic. My childhood memories are primarily composed of an alcoholic, former Marine Corps drill instructor father who, for the most part, may be labeled as an angry, verbally abusive, racist. The primary emotions I felt growing up were anger, disgust, and embarrassment toward him. As an only child, my regular home life activity was defending my mother from her drunken husband's abuse.

My first job, at the age of eight, was doing manual labor in my father's bar and restaurant; mostly bar with a little bit of restaurant. Over the next ten years, most of my money was earned from working various jobs at his bar: cleaning; sweeping, mopping, and scrubbing the tile floors in the kitchen once a week on my hands and knees, using nothing more than SOS pads and a bucket of scalding hot water; washing glasses, dishes, and pots and pans; cooking and serving tables; and later, tending bar and bouncing rowdy drunks out of the bar. On the major holidays like Thanksgiving and Christmas, when other kids were at home celebrating with their families, I was dealing with drunks at my father's bar.

I was a regular witness to the destructive effects of alcohol abuse and quickly found myself categorizing all alcohol-use as negative and destructive. If I had to summarize my early life experiences, it would be with the phrase "highly conflicted and emotionally detached." It was only my mother who made my home life bearable.

But, there is good news. At the age of seventeen, as a high school senior, I accepted Christ as my Savior and Lord due to the combined influence of my best friend Gary, Southeastern Wisconsin Youth for Christ, and the influence and encouragement of the ministry director Rev. Randy Barrows, as well as the various ministries of Racine Bible Church, in Racine, Wisconsin. Contributing to my spiritual growth were The Navigators discipleship ministry out of Colorado Springs, Colorado (*Design for Discipleship* Bible study workbooks), and Northwoods Youth Crusade/Fort Wilderness, in McNaughton, Wisconsin. The unexpectedly spectacular entrance of Christ into my life immediately and dramatically changed my heart and life goals. It also went a long way to healing the schism between me and my father. He accepted Christ fifteen years later, also dramatically transforming his life. It was a very real experience for him, both spiritually and emotionally. I am confident of his salvation and current home in heaven because of his dramatic and joyous emotional response at the moment he opened his heart to Christ. Joy was unknown to him prior to this emotionally tectonic event. This was quite a unique and telling testimony to the transforming power of Christ in the life of a former hardhearted, alcoholic Marine-turned-bar-owner.

When I committed my life to Christ, my negative and highly conflicted experiences with alcohol and alcohol abusers resulted in a dogmatic belief in the absolute evil of alcohol. In my mind a conviction emerged, that Christians should absolutely not drink alcohol under any conditions, and that alcohol use by a Christian represented sin, and was a sign of spiritual immaturity and inferiority. My judgmental spirit toward alcohol-using Christians was patently conspicuous.

But God had a special plan for me. God is the master of irony. He would lead me to Dallas Theological Seminary and later into the United States Army as an Army Chaplain, spending twenty-eight years in military ministry. As a retired Chaplain, I am now working for the Army as a Substance-Use Disorder Clinical Care Counseling Psychologist. Providing medical care and ministry to more than fifty soldiers suffering from substance-use disorders during an average work week is fairly common. To say God is the master of irony is, perhaps, the understatement of all time.

It is from these astonishing experiences this book emerged. The hand of God is clearly revealed on the path I have traveled so far in my life. Separated from the person and work of Christ, my life becomes incomprehensible and futile. God's continuous transforming work in my life is undeniable. The results of this book reflect His grace and mercy to me, as well as decades of emotional and spiritual growth. I thank Him daily for receiving that which I do not deserve. His grace and mercy have been boundless to me and to my father.

FOREWORD

by Dr. Ronald Boehme

You hold in your hands a remarkable book by a remarkable man that could radically change your life or that of a loved one.

I first heard the contents of this book in a doctoral dissertation oral exam where Guy Glad became "Dr. Glad" through a mesmerizing presentation. He left me feeling like the pupil, and extremely privileged to be the beneficiary of his research, heart, and the wisdom he shared on how people can intentionally break the alcohol habit.

My first thought after hearing his arguments was that *he needs to turn this superb piece of research into a book.*

I'm thrilled that he did.

Guy's military background and chaplaincy, and his work with recruits and officers as a Substance-Use Disorder Clinical Care Counseling Psychologist gives him a degree of knowledge that few people possess. Can you imagine an environment more susceptible to alcohol use/abuse than our armed forces, who are constantly in harm's way, often separated from their families, and faced with life and death situations?

I remember doing a chapel service years ago at one of the largest Army boot camps in the United States. The enlisted men and women seemed so vulnerable, homesick, and in need of someone or something to rouse their spirits—to believe. When I finished the message, they literally came running to the altar to find God and inner peace. Many of them had looked elsewhere to meet that need previously—with alcohol being the easiest escape.

But alcohol abuse is never an escape route—it's a devastating addiction that can not only take your own life from you (I'm sure you know friends who've damaged their livers as well as their souls), but negatively impact generations to come.

Guy Glad began his life in that environment. Miraculously, he overcame the scars of his family past to find answers, hope, and a passion for helping others find freedom.

I love the *balance* of his conclusions. He rightly points out that the Bible views alcohol (wine) as a blessing from God, an ancient offering made to God, and a curse we bring upon ourselves when moderate use diminishes. Dr. Glad is neither a teetotaler (don't drink at all), or a careless libertarian (it doesn't matter what you do).

He's a wise man who understands that if there is any area of life that needs advanced planning and intentionality, alcohol use fits the bill.

This book contains the history of alcohol use in human societies, powerful stories of changed lives, practical tips on kicking the habit, and resources that can help you when your resistance breaks down. I love the victorious worldview he presents, the many quotes and Bible verses that fill the pages, and the empathetic heart of a man who has seen the ugly side of alcohol and has cleverly designed a rope to help lift you out of the mud of self-destruction.

Grab on tightly, because the "Siren Song" in your heart comes to every human being. We all face temptations and oftentimes don't know what to do, where to turn.

Guy Glad points the way back to freedom and wholeness from alcohol abuse. And as he so wonderfully shares, it's the truth—about alcohol—that sets you free (John 8:32).

Drink thoughtfully and deeply from Dr. Glad's wellspring of knowledge on alcohol abuse. It may be one of the most important "sips" of knowledge you'll ever take.

1

—m—

Two-Way Vision

"Outward and Inward Looking"

Vigilance. The ultimate purpose of this book is to encourage Christians to "connect the spiritual dots" between the convergent issues of spiritual maturity and personal decisions regarding the use of alcohol. For some readers, it may seem inconceivable that this connection is not intuitive; yet, for some Christians, this connection has not yet become clear. Believers of all ages and degrees of spiritual maturity seem to have not given sufficient critical thinking to the issue of alcohol use for the Christian. It is my intent in writing this book to encourage biblically and evidence-based thinking within the church and to apply all divine revelation to the life-changing challenge to "think biblically" in personal decisions regarding alcohol use. Too many Christians are currently suffering in silence due to the comprehensively destructive effects of alcohol abuse in their lives, and that is nearly 10 percent of the church. For them, this book offers spiritual reconstruction and a new direction in life, catalyzed by the instruction embedded in God's natural and special revelation applied in the healing, guiding, comforting, and teaching hands of the Holy Spirit. The potential for positive change is high for Christians struggling with the physical, emotional, cognitive, and spiritual pillaging caused by alcohol abuse.

This book presents an objective, quantifiable method for making the important decision regarding alcohol use for the Christian. The basis of this decision-making method is similar to having "two-way vision."

Some dog breeds, primarily Pugs and Boston Terriers, possess an unusual eye condition called "Strabismus." This condition allows a dog's eyes to track different objects simultaneously. In other words, the dog can be looking at different objects in two different directions at the same time.[1]

---

1   "Strabismus," Wag, accessed December 27, 2018. https://wagwalking.com/condition/strabismus.

This is the idea behind the Christian having "two-way vision." Being able to view the subject of alcohol use through the lens of comprehensive truth and the condition of one's heart at the same time is a critical, spiritual life task. Metaphorically, this spiritual maturity task shares similarities with riding on a train. A person can ride on a train, looking at the passing scenery, while simultaneously being aware of the surroundings within the train. For the Christian, this represents possessing functional awareness of divine truth revealed in the surrounding world and within the Bible, while at the same time monitoring one's heart condition before God. Since both nature and the Bible have the fingerprints of God on them, it is God's expectation and desire for believers to respond to both equally (Psalm 19:1; Romans 1:20; Second Timothy 3:16-17).

Being able to make a connection between these two dynamics is essential for successful Christian living in general, and decisions regarding alcohol use in particular. This two-way vision will enable the believer to make the fullest use of God's revealed truth, biblically and from medicine and science, and apply this truth to one's life in an integrated fashion.

Looking Outward

Part of understanding truth in the world around us includes having an understanding of alcohol use and the history of the church. This is especially true of the Reformation, representing a critical period in world history.

The presence of alcohol permeates all of world history. Throughout history, alcohol has been present in different forms. Ranging from fermenting fruits in nature, to the human manufacture of alcoholic beverages, the presence and influence of alcohol has been clear and impactful. According to Narcotics Anonymous, "It's likely that alcohol production started when early farmers noted the fermentation that took place in fallen fruit. They may have found the fizzy flavor and sharp aroma pleasing. Trial and error using different fruits and grains finally resulted in formulas that could be refined and repeated for a pleasant alcoholic drink."[2] Inaba and Cohen note,

---

2   "Alcohol History," *Narcotics Anonymous,* accessed May 25, 2018, https://www. narconon.org/drug-information/alcohol-history.html.

Alcohol is the oldest and most widely used psychoactive drugs in the world. It has been around since airborne yeast spore fermented fruits and plants into alcohol about 1.5 billion years ago. Animals became drunk on alcohol long before humans did. Even today monkeys, giraffes, and elephants that eat the fermented fruit of the South African Marula tree after it has fallen to the ground get as staggeringly drunk as the most inebriated college freshman.[3]

Initially, mankind also imbibed and soon learned to manufacture alcoholic beverages. According to Curry,

All over the world, in fact, evidence for alcohol production from all kinds of crops is showing up, dating to near the dawn of civilization. University of Pennsylvania biomolecular archaeologist Patrick McGovern believes that's not an accident. From the rituals of the Stone Age on, he argues, the mind-altering properties of booze have fired our creativity and fostered the development of language, the arts, and religion. Look closely at great transitions in human history, from the origin of farming to the origin of writing, and you'll find a possible link to alcohol. "There's good evidence from all over the world that alcoholic beverages are important to human culture," McGovern says. "Thirty years ago, that fact wasn't as recognized as it is now."

Drinking is such an integral part of our humanity, according to McGovern, that he only half-jokingly suggests our species be called *Homo imbibens.*[4]

Smith and Seymour add their own humorous observations to the historical record of alcohol misuse in world history:

---

3   Darryl S. Inaba and William E. Cohen, *Uppers, Downers, All-Arounders: Physical and Mental Effects of Psychoactive Drugs* (Medford, OR: CNS Publications, 2011), 5.2.

4   Andrew Curry, "Our 9,000-Year Love Affair with Booze," *National Geographic*, accessed May 27, 2018, https://www.nationalgeographic.com/magazine/2017/02/ alcohol-discovery-addiction-booze-human-culture/.

The use of substances for the purpose of intoxication is far from new. In fact, it predates humanity and can still be found in animal behavior. Cedar waxwings and other birds are prone to ingestion of over-ripe Pyracanthus berries, after which they cavort and stagger around like a troop of soccer fans. The earliest human intoxicants were probably naturally fermented plant materials. One can imagine a cave-person sampling rotting fruit found under a tree and discovering that strange things happen in his or her perceptions. One can then imagine that cave person leading his or her fellows to the tree for the world's first cocktail party. One may assume that alcohol abuse followed that same afternoon. Addiction probably took a while.[5]

Besides the general, pre-flood biblical references to alcohol use (Matthew 24:38), the first specific biblical record of alcohol use was in the life of Noah, after the global flood of God's judgment upon sinful mankind. According to Comfort, et. al, "Noah was among the first to produce wine (Genesis 9:21), presumably on the slopes of Mount Ararat. But wine-making was not confined to that region, because Egypt, and later Greece, had a fondness for the juice. In fact, wine-making was known to have existed in the prehistoric period of Mesopotamia and was brought to Egypt before 3,000 B.C."[6]

Noah 's inspiring story of God's sovereignty and ultimate plan to bring salvation to the world is punctuated by intermittent times of failure and sadness. Among these times of sadness, the pages of the Bible reveal alcohol misuse that led to drunkenness and sin.

---

5   David E. Smith and Richard B. Seymour, *Clinician's Guide to Substance Abuse* (Chicago: McGraw-Hill Medical Publishing Division, 2001), 12.

6   Walter A. Elwell and Phillip W. Comfort. "Wine" in *Tyndale Bible Dictionary* (Wheaton, IL: Tyndale House Publishers, 2001), 1302.

Regarding this distressing time in Noah's life recorded in Genesis 9:20-22, Gil comments,

And he drank of the wine, and was drunken.... Either not being acquainted with the strength of it, as is thought by many; or having been used to weaker liquor, or water; or through the infirmity of his age; however, he was overtaken with it, which is recorded, not to disgrace him, but to caution men against the evil of intemperance, as well as to encourage repentant sinners to expect pardon. This shows that the best of men, yet not without sin, whereas he was a righteous man, he was not so by the righteousness of works, but by the righteousness of faith. And he was uncovered within his tent, and being in liquor when he laid down, he was either negligent of his long and loose garments, such as the Eastern people wore without breeches, and did not take care to wrap them about him; or in his sleep, through the heat of the weather, or of the wine, or both, threw them off.[7]

For purposes of clarity, in this book "alcohol" refers to a specific class of three alcohol types: wine, beer, and spirits. The common content of these alcoholic beverages is ethanol, a substance that is toxic to the human body if abused.[8] If ethanol sounds familiar to you, it is one of the main ingredients we put in the gas tank every time we fill up at the gas station. Kuhn, et al., explicate the history of alcohol use in the world with these incisive words:

---

7   John Gil, *Gil's Exposition of the Entire Bible* (Bible Hub: Internet Sacred Texts Archive), accessed May 27, 2018, http://biblehub.com/commentaries/gill/genesis/9.htm.

8   Cynthia Kuhn, Scott Swartzwelder, and Wilkie Wilson, Buzzed: *The Straight Facts About the Most Used and Abused Drugs from Alcohol to Ecstasy* (New York: W. W. Norton and Company, 2008), 34-36.

The use of chemicals to alter thinking and feeling is as old as humanity itself, and alcohol was probably one of the first substances used. Even the earliest historical writings make note of alcohol drinking, and breweries can be traced back some 6,000 years to ancient Egypt and Babylonia. In the Middle Ages, Arab technology introduced distillation as a way to increase the alcohol content in beverages to Europe. In those times, alcohol was believed to remedy practically any disease. In fact, the Gaelic term *whiskey* is best translated as "water of life." These days, alcoholic beverage is clearly the drug of choice for much of Western culture, and we need only to look closely at much of the advertising in this country to see that it is still sold as a magic elixir of sorts.[9]

Throughout world and biblical history, the dual nature of alcohol is clear. It has provided both pleasure and pain, enjoyment and turmoil. Abstinence or moderation appear to be the keys that unlock the door of lowering risks associated with alcohol use.

The history of the development of alcohol manufacture, culture, and even its own special language, is embedded with creativity and, in some cases, humor. For example, there are specialized and creative recipes for alcohol manufacture that transcend culture, geography, and time. Among the contributions to the English language are alcohol-related words like "moonshine" (brandy illegally smuggled in by moonlight), and "honeymoon" (referring to the custom of drinking alcohol for a month following a wedding).[10]

The following table provides an abbreviated summary of some key dates and events in the history of alcohol manufacture, legislation, and use in the world:

---

9   Ibid., 36.

10   "History of Alcohol Use," academics.lmu.edu, accessed May 26, 2018, https://academics.lmu.edu/headsup/forstudents/historyofalcoholuse/.

Table 1: Key Events in History Regarding Alcohol

Date	Key Events
6000-4000 BC	Viticulture proliferates (tailored cultivation of grapes for use in making wine), originating in what is now modern Armenia.
3000-2000 BC	Beer making in what is now modern Iraq, resulting in more than 20 recipes recorded on clay tablets. Wine trade in the Mediterranean region increases.
2200 BC	Cuneiform tablet recommends beer to relieve lactating women.
3000-1000 BC	Beer remains unrefined and must be drunk through a straw due to the large amounts of grain and mash in it. Beer production increased in northern Syria.
1500 BC	Wine produced commercially in the Mediterranean region.
900-800 BC	Extensive commercial vineyards in what is now modern Iraq produced more than 10,000 wineskins for the capitol of Nimrod.
800 BC	Distillation of barley and rice beer takes place in India.
50 BC	Dionysius of Halicarnassus writes, "the Gauls (French) have no knowledge of wine…but use a foul-smelling liqueur made of barley rotted in water (beer)."
500 AD	Wine-making reaches China. First reference made to the use of hops in beer.
1100 AD	First medical reference to the product of distillation of wine as "spirits" by the medical school at Salerno, Italy.
1516 AD	New German Purity Law dictates beer is made only with barley, hops, and pure water.

1550-1575 AD	Widespread drunkenness documented in England, now considered a crime, with new evolving laws created to counter inebriation. For the next two centuries drunkenness negatively impacts all areas of life in England.
1606 AD	In England, Parliament passes a new law against inebriation called "The Act to Repress the Odious and Loathsome Sin of Drunkenness."
17th Century	American laws are passed to battle drunkenness, while at the same time making laws to facilitate the sale and distribution of alcohol in Massachusetts.
1643 AD	England taxes alcohol, triggering production of homemade moonshine.
1650-1675 AD	Various laws in the New England colonies created to define drunkenness and control the production, distribution, and use of alcohol.
1700-1948 AD	Expansion of new types of alcohol; creation of laws to suppress drunkenness; expansion of the manufacture, distribution, and use of alcohol worldwide; Prohibition and its repeal in America; President Carter signs a bill legalizing the home brewing of beer in 1978.[11].

As a reflection of world history and the surrounding culture, the dualistic blessing and curse of alcohol has likewise been present for God's people throughout biblical history. Following Noah 's first incident of alcohol misuse (Genesis 9:20-22) are scores of warnings and guidance regarding the blessing and curse of alcohol use.

On one hand, we discover encouragement to use wine to cheer the soul or improve health, being seen as a blessing from God, or to be utilized as an offering to God. On the other hand, alcohol abuse is summarily condemned throughout the Bible as an egregious sin.

---

11   Ibid.

Alcohol use

The idea that alcohol use for the Christian is acceptable, while abuse is condemned, is not new. Renowned Christian philosopher, theologian, and scholar C. S. Lewis, makes this point with these insightful words in his discussion on "The Cardinal Virtues:"

> Temperance referred not specially to drink, but to all pleasures, and it meant not abstaining, but *going the right length and no further.* It is a mistake to think that Christian's ought all to be teetotalers. Mohammedanism, not Christianity, is the teetotal religion. Of course, it may be the duty of a particular Christian, or of any Christian, at a particular time, to abstain from strong drink, either because he is the sort of man who cannot drink at all without drinking too much, or because he is with people who are inclined to drunkenness and must not encourage them by drinking himself. But the whole point is that he is abstaining for a good reason, from something which he does not condemn and which he likes to see other people enjoying. One of the marks of a certain type of bad man is that he cannot give up a thing himself without wanting everyone else to give it up. That is not the Christian way. An individual Christian may see fit to give up all sorts of things for special reasons, whether marriage, or meat, or beer, or the cinema, but the moment he starts saying the things are bad in themselves or looking down his nose at other people who do use them, he has taken the wrong turning (emphasis mine).[12]

Hence, if an individual Christian makes the decision to use alcohol, the "lynchpin understanding" appears to revolve around how much one should drink or, more specifically, what are my limits regarding alcohol use, limits that keep me safe and low risk, versus going beyond this limit and entering into territory that is characterized with lack of control, probable destruction to health, relationships, career, finances, spiritual life, and high-risk decision-making.

---

12 C. S. Lewis, *The Complete C. S. Lewis Signature Classics* (San Francisco: Harper Collins Publishers, 2002), 49.

Looking Inward

This concept of engaging "two-way vision" for successful Christian living regarding decisions about alcohol use demands an honest look into my heart. Honestly assessing my spiritual and emotional condition is a catalyzing requirement for alcohol-use decisions for the Christian. This candid self-assessment elicits further questions like:

- What do I believe is my purpose in life?
- What place does God have in my planning and motivation for my life?
- How important and relevant is the Bible in my daily life and decisions?
- What is the relationship between the holiness of God and daily decisions I make?

A concise understanding and application of these questions to my life is a crucial component of my spiritual growth, maturity, and decisions regarding alcohol-use.

My purpose in life

Understanding my purpose in life will function like a rudder functions on a sailing ship; it provides a metaphorical azimuth to the compass of life. It will give direction to all of my decisions, foci, and emphases. The importance of ensuring my moral azimuth is accurate cannot be overstated. When using a map and compass for hiking, land navigation, or general traveling, it is crucial to get the beginning degree, the azimuth, correct. Even a one-degree error in direction turns into a massive error ten miles down the road. This is a major life lesson, that a very small error in direction initially turns into being way off course as the journey progresses. For example, if I look at a map that shows me where the starting point of a trip is, I must also understand the concept of "true north" in order to ensure my trip will end in success. Even a small starting error will negatively impact the finish line. This principle applies to all spiritual and moral areas of life, including the Christian's decision regarding alcohol use.

So, what is the purpose in life for every Christian? The Bible is clear about this purpose. Paul provides this succinct exhortation in First Corinthians 10:31 with these words: "So whether you eat or drink, or whatever you do, do it all for the glory of God." The concept of "the glory of God " is not some mystical concept that we somehow miraculously discover in a lifetime of search, and trial and error. The Bible is unequivocal on this point. The glory of God is honored in my life when I seek to obey His revealed will in the Bible in every decision I make. The apostle John clearly reflects this principle in First John 5:3 with these incisive words: "Loving God means keeping his commandments, and his commandments are not burdensome." MacArthur goes a step further when he declares that all the commands of the Bible can be summed up in five specific directives for the Christian's lifetime focus: (1) to be saved, (2) to be sanctified, (3) to be submissive, (4) to be Spirit-filled, and (5) to be willing to suffer for the sake of Christ. He concludes with these words:

> Okay, let me give you the final principle, but hold on to your seat. You may want to jump up and shout. If you are doing all five of the basic things, do you know what the next principle of God's will is? *Do whatever you want.* If these five elements of God's will are operating in your life, who is running your wants? God is. The psalmist said, "Delight yourself in the Lord; and He will give you the desire of your heart " (Psalm 37:4). God does not say He will fulfill all the desires there. If you are living a godly life, He will give you the right desires.[13]

My motivation in life

Emerging out of a clear understanding of my purpose in life will be an overarching motivation. For many, the energizing motivation in life may rest in money, fame, promotion, or relationships. However, an accurately grounded, biblically based life purpose will establish and catalyze my life motivation.

The Bible is unambiguous regarding God's intended motivation for Christians. Paul states our overarching motivation in life must be

---

13 John MacArthur, *Found: God's Will* (Colorado Springs, CO: David C. Cook, 2012), 67-68.

the glory of God (First Corinthians 10:31). He adds that "the measure of the stature of the fullness of Christ" should be a corollary life goal for the believer (Ephesians 4:13). Proverbs presents this life goal as "the pursuit of wisdom." More specifically, the application of biblical wisdom to all areas of life, and the express goal of avoiding folly and destructive decisions, is the theme weaving its way throughout the book. Proverbs 1:2-7 summarizes this goal and the purpose of the entire book:

> [2] for gaining wisdom and instruction; for
>   understanding words of insight;
> [3] for receiving instruction in prudent behavior,
>   doing what is right and just and fair;
> [4] for giving prudence to those who are simple,
>   knowledge and discretion to the young
> [5] let the wise listen and add to their learning,
>   and let the discerning get guidance
> [6] for understanding proverbs and parables,
>   the sayings and riddles of the wise.
> [7] The fear of the Lord is the beginning of knowledge,
>   but fools despise wisdom and instruction.

We are told in this passage this pursuit of wisdom begins with the fear of the Lord and continues throughout life, being reminded that fools despise this journey. The application of biblical wisdom must also

be directed to decisions regarding alcohol use. In this regard, Proverbs is clear: there is a way that leads to life (the way of wisdom), and a way that leads to death (the way of folly). According to Buzzell, "… wisdom in the Old Testament often refers to the mental and physical skills of craftsmen, sailors, singers, mourners, administrators, counselors, and others; but other times, as in Proverbs, it focuses on the application of moral and ethical principles that result in skillful, godly living."[14] There is no gray area here. My decision regarding alcohol use may be considered wise or foolish. And wisdom must always be the path of choice as my motivation in life (Proverbs 9:9-10; 15:33; 18:5).

My compass in life

The Bible stands as the ultimate authoritative compass for Christians. It is incumbent on every Christian to know the Bible well enough to understand the critical importance of applying it to every area of life, including decisions regarding alcohol use. The central biblical teaching about its nature and function is Second Timothy 3:16-17: "All Scripture is inspired by God and is useful to teach us what is true and to make us realize what is wrong in our lives. It corrects us when we are wrong and teaches us to do what is right. God uses it to prepare and equip his people to do every good work." The biblical functions of teaching, reproof, correction, and training represent comprehensive tools for spiritual growth and positive progress in the spiritual maturity process. According to Lea and Griffin,

> Paul focused on three contributions Scripture can provide for the believer. The Scriptures contain the explanation of God's plan of salvation (v. 15). They contain an outline of doctrine and truth that support the plan of salvation (v. 16). The Scriptures also provide warning to keep Christians from wandering afield from God's will. Those who obey the commands and respond to the promises of Scripture can find the strength to live a life of such arresting quality that it can encourage and enlighten others.[15]

In this sense, the Bible represents our lifetime compass, providing correct directions for all decisions, including the Christian's view of, and decisions regarding alcohol use.

---

14 S. S. Buzzell, "Proverbs." In J. F. Walvoord & R. B. Zuck, eds., *The Bible Knowledge Commentary: An Exposition of the Scriptures*, Vol. 1 (Wheaton, IL: Victor Books. 1985), 907.

15 T. D. Lea and H. P. Griffin, *1, 2 Timothy, Titus*, Vol. 34 (Nashville: Broadman & Holman Publishers, 1992), 238.

Another metaphor used in the Bible to describe its function is that of a "lamp." Psalm 119:97-105 reminds us of this with these words:

[97] Oh, how I love your law. I meditate on it all day long.
[98] Your commands are always with me and
make me wiser than my enemies.
[99] I have more insight than all my teachers,
for I meditate on your statutes.
[100] I have more understanding than the
elders, for I obey your precepts.
[101] I have kept my feet from every evil path so
that I might obey your word.
[102] I have not departed from your laws, for
you yourself have taught me.
[103] How sweet are your words to my taste,
sweeter than honey to my mouth.
[104] I gain understanding from your precepts;
therefore I hate every wrong path.
[105] Your word is a lamp for my feet, a light on my path (NIV).

This classic Psalm addresses the question "How can a young person stay on the path of purity?" The immediate answer is "By living according to your word" (119:9 NIV)." The protective and enlightening nature of the Bible in the life of the obedient Christians is a common theme that weaves its way throughout the pages of Scripture. For the Christian, understanding and abiding by biblical principles and commands, of both commission and omission, is a critical spiritual growth task that must be targeted as a rigorous, daily discipline. And this includes decisions regarding alcohol use.

My mirror in life

When you look in the mirror, what do you expect to see? We all know (sometimes painfully) that what we see is the exact reflection of reality. The only exception to this is when one goes to the circus and wanders through the house of mirrors, all of which are designed to give skewed and humorous views of one's body. But life is not a circus, and what we see in the mirror tells us everything we want to know about how we look.

The Christian life is also intended to be a kind of mirror. Ideally, the Christian life is designed to mirror the holiness and character of God. Realistically, we will never perfectly reflect God's holiness and character. However, as a life goal and "spiritual ruler" that measures the fruit evident in the Christian's life, the holiness and character of God also establish the ground from which all decisions in life must emerge. Peter reflects this truth in First Peter 1:15-16 with this command: "But now you must be holy in everything you do, just as God who chose you is holy. For the Scriptures say, 'You must be holy because I am holy'". This divine expectation for God's children is a recurrent, major theme, revealed more than twenty-five times throughout the Bible. The book of Leviticus presents a clear snapshot of the idea of God's holiness necessarily being reflected in believers' lives:

Leviticus 20:7: "Consecrate yourselves and be holy, because I am the Lord your God."

Leviticus 19:2: "Speak to the entire assembly of Israel and say to them: 'Be holy because I, the Lord your God, am holy.'"

Leviticus 11:44-45: "I am the Lord your God; consecrate yourselves and be holy, because I am holy. Do not make yourselves unclean by any creature that moves along the ground. I am the Lord, who brought you up out of Egypt to be your God; therefore be holy, because I am holy."

According to Raymer:

Rather as obedient children (lit. "children of obedience") they were to mold their characters to "be holy" in all they did" (First Peter 1:15). Their lifestyle was to reflect not their former ignorance (*agnoia*), but the holy (*hagioi*) nature of their heavenly Father who gave them new birth and called them (cf. "called" in Second Peter 1:3) to be His own. First Peter 1:15-16 do not speak of legal requirements but are a reminder of a Christian's responsibility in his inner life and outer walk. Though absolute holiness can never be achieved in this life, all areas of life should be in the process of becoming completely conformed to God's perfect and holy will.[16]

---

16 R. M. Raymer, "First Peter." In J. F. Walvoord and R. B. Zuck, eds., *The Bible Knowledge Commentary: An Exposition of the Scriptures,* Vol. 2 (Wheaton, IL: Victor Books, 1985), 843.

So when you review the reflection your life gives back to you, what do you see? Is it a reflection of God's holiness and your desire to progressively become more like Him, or something else? The reflection of the Christian life must be the holiness of God, including decisions surrounding alcohol use.

A Success Story

Nicholas was a twenty-four-year-old military member who had been serving for two years. Through the local ministry of a para-church group Bible study he came to Christ six months earlier. He attended a two-hour spiritual growth seminar that addressed the specific relationship between spiritual maturity and alcohol-use decisions for Christians. The seminar presented medical and scientific principles of alcohol use and the dangers of developing alcohol-use disorders (general revelation), and biblical principles of alcohol-use and spiritual growth (special revelation). The seminar had a clear emotional and spiritual impact on Nicholas. During one feedback session at the end of the training, Nicholas shared the following response: "I have been a Christian now for six months. I have also been engaging in excessive alcohol use. This has been a burden on me and until this seminar I went to social gatherings just hoping I wouldn't drink too much. But now I have learned I can put a number to how much I am going to drink (no more than three standard drinks), and not have to worry about getting drunk. If I decide to drink now I no longer have to measure my alcohol use based on how much everybody else around me is drinking. I wish I had known these principles six months ago."

Critical Thought
Focusing on God's revealed truth in the Bible, and in creation, will function as a lifetime compass for you to follow

Questions for Further Thought

1. *What is your belief regarding the relationship between spiritual maturity and alcohol use?*

2. *Can you prove this belief biblically?*

3. *Do you know what medical science asserts regarding alcohol use?*

4. *Do you have an objective, quantifiable number that represents the boundary between alcohol use and abuse?*

5. *What is this definition based on?*

2

Viewing a Multifaceted Diamond

"The Unity of Truth"

Integration. Throughout the process of connecting spiritual maturity to alcohol use decisions, worldview is the fulcrum for change and growth. For the Christian, worldview deals with the interaction between, and integration of, all truth, in order to live the most effective, fruitful, and successful life possible, ultimately for the glory of God. This involves adopting, developing, and applying a Christian worldview that considers both the Bible, as the special revelation from God, and creation, as God's general revelation regarding natural truth. This includes the dynamics surrounding alcohol use. John MacArthur offers this definition of a Christian worldview:

> The Christian worldview sees and understands God the Creator and His creation, that is, man and the world, primarily through the lens of God's special revelation, the Holy Scriptures, and secondarily through God's natural revelation in creation as interpreted by human reason and reconciled by and with Scripture, for the purpose of believing and behaving in accord with God's will and thereby, glorifying God with one's mind and life.[1]

Developing a spiritually sound worldview creates a "way of wisdom" thinking pattern. For too long, decisions surrounding the use of alcohol for Christians have been relegated to being a matter of opinion, hope ("I hope I don't drink too much tonight."), comparison ("How much is everybody else drinking … I guess this is normal."), or conjecture ("I think

---

1   John MacArthur, *Think Biblically: Recovering a Christian Worldview* (Wheaton, IL: Crossway Books, 2003), 14.

I know what my limit is."). Hence, this subjectivism is the culprit behind alcohol abuse and the reprehensible sin of drunkenness. An objective and quantifiable boundary between alcohol use versus abuse is desperately needed in both the contemporary culture and the church. More about this quantifiable boundary later.

Historically, Christian apologists and theologians have defined two specific domains of truth; general revelation (nature), and special revelation (the Bible). Others have christened these twin categories of truth as natural theology and biblical theology. According to Boyce,

> Natural theology embraces what man may attain by the study of God in nature. This extends not only to what is beheld of him in the Heavens and the Earth, but also in the intellectual and spiritual nature of man himself … Biblical theology consists in the facts of the Bible, harmonized by scriptural comparison, generalized by scriptural theories, crystalized into scriptural doctrines, and so systematized as to show the system of truth taught, to the full extent that it is a system, and no farther.[2]

The concept of the unity of truth establishes that truth from both domains is a part of the overarching arena of God's truth. While there is some semantic disagreement with this definition of the unity of truth, it is generally understood and accepted by most Christian scholars. Swain explains the clear but related distinction between general and special revelation:

> General revelation refers to that which God makes known through creation to all rational creatures (Psalm 19:1-6; Romans 1:19-20). In general revelation, our knowledge proceeds from creation to its creator. The artwork leads us to the artist … In special revelation, the Creator of all things addresses us personally. The artist reveals himself to us. The knowledge of God available through special revelation far exceeds what is available through general revelation in both content and efficacy.[3]

2 James P. Boyce, *Abstract of Systematic Theology* (Louisville, KY: Low Tide Press, 1887), https://archive.org/stream/abstractofsystem00boyc#page/n5/mode/2up.

3 Scott R. Swain, "Revelation," in *Systematic Theology Study Bible* (Wheaton, IL: Crossway Books, 2017), 1664.

The philosophic key to the concept of the unity of truth is balance. According to Mayhue, "The proper balance comes by beginning with Scripture, which is inerrant. Where the Bible speaks to a discipline, its truth is superior. When the Bible does not speak, there is a whole world of God's creation to explore for knowledge, but with the caveat that man's ability to draw conclusions is fallible, unlike God's Word."[4]

General revelation pertains to the realm of evidence-based observations and biblically supported conclusions regarding nature. According to Psalm 19:1, "The heavens proclaim the glory of God. The skies display his craftsmanship". In combination with medical science, it is within the natural science of Physics we can see the truth of natural revelation most clearly. The impressive discoveries of Physics range from the physical law behind how a boomerang works (from 20,000 B.C.), to the natural laws governing particle physics, and the object of study of the Large Hadron Collider (from 2009 A.D.). Even a curveball thrown by a baseball pitcher obeys certain natural laws.[5]

None of these laws is found in the Bible. Yet they are still true, and represent a reflection of God's creative design. Matthew Henry provides the following insight regarding Psalm 19:1, and the concept of general revelation: "The heavens so declare the glory of God, and proclaim his wisdom, power, and goodness, that all ungodly men are left without excuse. They speak themselves to be the works of God's hands; for they must have a Creator who is eternal, infinitely wise, powerful, and good."[6] Bloesch states that creation contains the "refracted light of the glory of God " and that "there is a universal reflection of God in creation.[7] In other words, design demands a designer, and truth inherent in the design reflects the designer's truth.

---

4   Richard L. Mayhue, "Cultivating a Biblical Mind-Set." In *Think Biblically: Recovering a Christian Worldview*, 51.

5   Clifford A. Pickover, *The Physics Book* (New York: Barnes & Noble, 2011).

6   Matthew Henry, *Matthew Henry's Bible Commentary*, Christianity.com, accessed May 28, 2018.https://www.christianity.com/bible/commentary.php?com=mhc&b=19&c=19.

7   Donald G. Bloesch, *Holy Scripture: Revelation, Inspiration & Interpretation* (Downers Grove, IL: InterVarsity Press, 1994), 74.

Special revelation is generally limited to, and emerges out of, biblical content. The activating and energizing principles of biblical authority and inerrancy serve as the foundation of special revelation. Paul reflects this principle in Second Timothy 3:16-17 when he declares, "All Scripture is inspired by God and is useful to teach us what is true, and to make us realize what is wrong in our lives. It corrects us when we are wrong and teaches us to do what is right. God uses it to prepare and equip his people to do every good work". The pivotal hermeneutical emphasis within these verses resides in the word "inspired." The original Greek word used here is "θεøπνευστος," (*theopneustos,* literally "God-breathed").[8] This uniquely specialized word appears only here in the New Testament. Ryrie notes, "… the Bible came from God through the men who wrote it. God superintended these human authors so that, using their individual personalities, they composed and recorded, without error, God's Word to man. Christ attested to the fact that inspiration extends to the very words (Matthew 5:18; John 10:35).[9]

MacArthur adds, "So identified is God with His Word that when Scripture speaks, God speaks."[10] In his tirelessly monumental research and writing regarding the trustworthiness and nature of the Bible, McDowell notes that the words of the Bible, all of them, have been inspired by God and cannot be ignored or marginalized. He states, "The process of inspiration extended to every word ('all Scripture') refuting the idea of myth and error. Since God is behind the writings, and since He is perfect, the result must be infallible. If it were not infallible, we would be left with God-inspired error."[11] Wallace observes that the grammatical construction of this verse indicates the purpose and result of God's Word in the Christian life.[12]

---

8   Robert Young, *Analytical Concordance to the Bible* (Grand Rapids, MI: Eerdmans Publishing Company, 1975), 512.

9   Charles C. Ryrie, *The Ryrie Study Bible* (Chicago: Moody Press, 1978), notes on Second Timothy 3:16.

10   John MacArthur, *The MacArthur Study Bible* (Nashville: Word Bibles, 1997), notes on Second Timothy 3:16.

11   Josh McDowell, *A Ready Defense* (San Bernardino, CA: Here's Life Publishers, Inc, 1992), 174.

12   Daniel B. Wallace, *Greek Grammar Beyond the Basics: An Exegetical Syntax of the New Testament* (Grand Rapids, MI: Zondervan Publishing House, 1996), 380.

This principle, the inerrant, infallible, and authoritative Bible, under-girds this book. Geisler declares, "…the Bible bears the fingerprints of God."[13] Chafer loudly echoes the preceding line of testimony regarding the character and authority of the Bible, declaring, "The primary character of the Bible is such as to lend it authority. It speaks as the voice of Him who created all things and to whom all things belong. To those who believe the Bible and heed its precepts it becomes an unerring lamp unto the feet and a light unto the path (Psalm 119:105). The Word of God fails not."[14]

Achieving balance regarding the concept of the unity of truth provides impetus for effective spiritual growth and timely ministry. Cheydleur notes:

> In 1994 the American Psychiatric Association (APA) updated its diagnostic criteria for alcohol-related problems in a way that clearly differentiates among alcohol intoxication, abuse, and dependency. This is particularly helpful for pastors and other Christian workers who seek to understand how the sin of drunkenness and the disease of alcoholism relate to each other.[15]

The APA updated these diagnostic criteria in 2013 in the *Diagnostic and Statistical Manual of Mental Health Disorders*, 5th edition.

An understanding, integration, and application of general and special revelation regarding decisions about the use of alcohol provides a balance, enabling personal health and blessing as the direct result of Christian spiritual maturity. While it is historically true that an element of the church has viewed science with suspicion,[16] this integrated balance regarding the unity of truth presents a source of confidence for Christians. Grudem confidently asserts:

---

13 Norman Geisler, *Systematic Theology*, Vol. 1 (Minneapolis: Bethany House, 2002), 252.

14 Lewis Sperry Chafer, *Systematic Theology*, Vol. VII (Dallas: Dallas Seminary Press, 1947), 46.

15 J. R. Cheydleur, "Alcohol-Induced Disorders," in *Baker Encyclopedia of Psychology & Counseling*, 2nd ed. (Grand Rapids, MI: Baker Books, 1999), 60.

16 Gary B. Ferngren, *Science & Religion: A Historical Introduction* (London: Johns Hopkins University Press, 2002), 264.

We should not fear to investigate scientifically the facts of the created world but should do so eagerly and with complete honesty, confident that when facts are rightly understood they will always turn out to be consistent with God's inerrant words in Scripture. Similarly, we should approach the study of Scripture eagerly and with confidence that, when rightly understood, Scripture will never contradict facts in the natural world.[17]

McMinn and Campbell add, "Though both Christian theology and science call for humility, they rely on different external standards; special revelation for the theologian and general revelation for the scientist. But to the Christian, both are legitimate forms of revelation, so we need not fear either the methods or findings of science."[18] These two domains of truth cannot be maintained as autonomous but applied in an integrated fashion.[19]

Nature demonstrates the character of God and His design; the Bible encapsulates the definition of spiritual maturity, providing the wisdom and guidance necessary when making alcohol-use decisions. The foundational element of these (or any) principles or beliefs is the concept of the unity of truth. Simply put, the unity of truth posits that all truth is God's truth. Regardless of source, if something is empirically and objectively true, then it is rooted and grounded in the domain of God's truth. Thomas summarizes the historical division that has existed between biblical and natural truth with these words,

...we are brought face to face with the antitheses of Revelation and discovery, of revelation and speculation, of Revelation and evolution; and while accepting to the full all historical processes,

---

17 Wayne Grudem, *Systematic Theology: An Introduction to Biblical Doctrine* (Grand Rapids, MI: Zondervan, 1994), 275.

18 Mark R. McMinn and Clark D. Campbell, *Integrative Psychotherapy: Toward a Comprehensive Christian Approach* (Downers Grove, IL: IVP Academic, 2007), 57.

19 Stanley Hauerwas, "Salvation and Health: Why Medicine Needs the Church," in *On Moral Medicine: Theological Perspectives in Medical Ethics*, 2nd ed. Stephen E. Lammers and Allen Verhey, eds. (Grand Rapids, MI: William B. Eerdmans Publishing Company, 1998), 75.

we are led to the conviction that, (1) Christianity is only adequately explained as a personal revelation of God, who used and guided history for this purpose; and (2) that history, discovery, philosophy, and evolution are simply the means or channels by which the Revelation has come.[20]

A word of caution regarding extra-biblical truth. The essence of science and medicine is continuing research and evolving information. In his early work with alcoholism, Jellinek presents a concise summary of the philosophical conflict that existed for the past few centuries between those embracing the view of alcoholism as a disease, versus those viewing alcoholism through the lens of a non-disease condition of "inebriety.[21]

Regardless of etiological lens, alcohol addiction clearly presents with symptoms that are progressive, plainly implying that current non-biblical truth may not be eternal truth. This is one lesson emerging out of the historically significant studies of Jellinek, demonstrating how scientific studies morph over time. This fact necessitates the requirement to "test all things" (First Thessalonians 5:21) in order to determine if any supposed truth violates any eternal truth (i.e., the Bible). Chafer reinforces this caution with these words: "No small problem is confronted when an attempt is made to state scientific truth according to the understanding of one age in a way that will at the same time be acceptable in all succeeding ages. Science is ever shifting and subject to its own revisions, if not complete revolutions."[22]

The unity of truth is the cornerstone of Christian analyses of extra-biblical subjects. This is an appropriate lens through which to view evidence-based medical truth regarding alcohol use, and the development and progress of alcohol-related disorders. And this medical evidence is a critical component of spiritually mature decisions regarding the use of alcohol for Christians. St. Augustine famously declared, "All truth is God's

---

20 W. H. Griffith Thomas, "The Principles of Theology: Introduction to the ThirtyNine Articles," accessed May 31, 2018. http://www.preachershelp.net/wp-content/ uploads/2014/11/griffith-thomas-39-articles.pdf

21 E. M. Jellinek, *The Disease Concept of Alcoholism* (Mansfield Centre, CT: Martino Publishing, 2010), 1-12.

22 Lewis Sperry Chafer, *Systematic Theology*, Vol. I (Dallas: Dallas Seminary Press, 1974), 34.

truth."[23]This statement refers to all truth about God, His creation, natural processes reflected in His handiwork, and that are true of Him and His character. Stanford observes:

> The Scriptures teach us who God is and who we are, but their purpose is not to give us *all* factual truth. For instance, they can't tell us how our heart or liver work…the Bible is not a science book, nor is it a manual on how to fix your car…the way the heart functions, the process by which a seed grows into a mature plant, and the fact that the earth is in an elliptical orbit around the sun are all truths based in the creative power and majesty of God (Romans 1:20)…God's majesty is reflected on how our brain cells function, the biological and environmental factors that affect the formation of our personalities, the mechanism by which memories are brought to our minds, and the precise balance of brain chemicals that are the foundation of our thoughts and behaviors. So, we must be like the Bereans, ever examining the Scriptures (Acts 17:11) as we look at the interplay between psychology, psychiatry, and faith.[24]

It is precisely the unity of truth principle upon which this section hinges; to illuminate the negative effects alcohol misuse has upon one's life, including the physical organs of the body as outlined in the above citation, in order to make spiritually mature decisions regarding alcohol use. Alcohol misuse has catastrophic health consequences depending upon frequency and intensity of use. These consequences will be discussed later in this book.

---

23 Matthew S. Stanford, *Grace for the Afflicted: A Clinical and Biblical Perspective on Mental Illness* (Downers Grove: IL: InterVarsity Press, 2017), 40.
24 Ibid.

A Growth Story

Ralph was a senior leader in his organization now for eighteen years, having attained many promotions through the ranks, gaining with it much responsibility. He reported being a Christian but admitted he had not been "living that life" for quite a while now, especially regarding his alcohol use. Ralph discussed his recent history of alcohol use, clearly describing abuse on an almost nightly basis for the past two years. As time progressed in therapy, Ralph was encouraged more and more to begin focusing on, and nurturing his emaciated spiritual maturity. He began attending church and men's Bible study, regularly engaging in personal devotions on an increasing basis, and intentionally attending men's retreats. Over time, Ralph's spiritual growth became a protective factor in his life, giving him the strength to make it through his intense cravings. Nearly a year passed, and his recovery continued. One day in group therapy he shared the following: "I never realized how important it is to know and apply the Bible to my life along with what medical science says about alcohol use disorders. My life has been saved, along with my family, and my future."

Critical Thought

A proper understanding and balanced integration of special and general revelation will provide invaluable wisdom and insight for living the Christian life.

Questions for Further Thought

1. What "system of truth" do you follow as the moral compass of your life?

2. What is the authority behind this system of truth?

3. What are the ways you believe God communicates with you?

4. Have any of the decisions you ever made in your life turned out to violate biblical teaching? If so, what were the results?

5. Is there any area in your life currently not in compliance with biblical teaching? What about your view of alcohol use?

The following three biblically based principles are foundational to the connection between Christian spiritual maturity regarding alcohol-use decisions.

Know Your Enemy

"Understanding Alcohol Use Disorders"

Understand. Understanding the impact of alcohol and ensuing alcohol use disorders that result from misuse is crucial for making healthy alcohol-use decisions. Porter notes, "Alcohol consumption and alcoholism is made up of the chemical, physical, physiological, and psychological effects that alcohol has on human beings, and the accumulative impact of these effects."[25]A comprehensive study of the history, composition, effects, and limits of alcohol and alcohol use is provided by Inaba and Cohen.[26] It is only through evidence-based research that we can understand these dynamics, an understanding that is rooted and grounded in a definitive description of the boundary between alcohol use and misuse.[27]

Today the widely accepted model of alcoholism is the Disease, or Medical Model.[28] However, there is disagreement regarding the generally accepted model of alcoholism as a disease. The early doubts of Jellinek in this regard are well-documented, while other contemporary researchers and scholars point to the reward center of the human brain as the key to a proper understanding of addiction *not* as a disease. According to Lewis:

Every experience that is repeated enough times because of its motivational appeal will change the wiring of the striatum (and related regions of the brain), while adjusting the flow and uptake of dopamine. Yet we wouldn't want to call the excitement we feel when visiting Paris, meeting a lover, or cheering for our favorite team a disease. Each rewarding experience builds its own network

---

25 William Porter, *Alcohol Explained* (nc: William Porter, nd), 5. Also available online at:https://www.goodreads.com/book/show/25374689-alcohol-explained.

26 Darryl S. Inaba and William E. Cohen, *Uppers, Downers, All-Arounders: Physical and Mental Effects of Psychoactive Drugs* (Medford, OR: CNS Publications, 2011), 5.1-5.45.

27 Mitch Earleywine, *Substance Use Problems* (Cambridge, MA: Hogrefe & Huber Publishers, 2009).

28 Marc Lewis, *The Biology of Desire* (New York: Public Affairs, 2015), 11.

of synapses in and around the striatum, and these networks continue to draw dopamine from its reservoir in the midbrain.[29]

Others place a heavy emphasis on sin, and the disintegration of the human brain, due to alcohol misuse, as the primary reason for alcohol-use disorders. Thompson asserts: From a neuroscience perspective, sin is deeply reflected in the degree to which our minds are disintegrated, or in Paul's language, depraved. In other words, what the language of neuroscience calls disintegration offers a correlate to the scriptural language of sin. Neuroscience also has something to tell us about turning away from sin. When we pay attention to our minds we can begin to stop the disintegration and embrace the acts of confession and repentance that lead to redemption. No wonder then, that Paul links regeneration with the healing, or integration, of the mind (Romans 12:1-2).[30]

These observations, while based in neuroscience, reflect the Spiritual Model of Addiction. This model places a great deal of emphasis on avoidance of sinful behavior, repentance of sin when it occurs, and an intentional desire to obey God and His Word every day, in all decisions, including decisions regarding alcohol use.

The insidious and eroding degenerative effects alcohol misuse has on the human body, and, secondarily, every area of life, is reflected in the word *progressive*. The progressive and deceptive nature of alcohol-use disorders may be described with a military term: *mission creep*. This is a reference to the slow but dramatic change from one condition to another that is not immediately or clearly seen until the change is complete. The creeping, progressive nature of alcohol-use disorders is both predictable and dynamic; its character and stages are described by evidence-based medical science, summarized in the following list:

1. They produce an altered mood state such as sedation, relaxation, or euphoria.
2. These effects reinforce the drug use; that is, the feelings aroused by the drug make the user want to use it again.

---

29   Ibid, 163.
30   Curt Thompson, *Anatomy of the Soul* (Carol Stream, IL: Tyndale House Publishers, 2010), 184.

3. Compulsive use occurs; the user feels as though he must have the drug.

4. Use continues despite the known, harmful effects. Many alcoholics, for example, continue to drink despite severe, irreversible liver damage.

5. Regular and temporal patterns of use occur. Drug users tend to use drugs on a regular basis and at specific times during the day.

6. Deprivation increases desire to use.

7. Paired stimuli increases use.[31]

8. Tolerance develops. More and more alcohol is required in order to create the same effects.

9. Physical dependence may develop; that is, regular, prolonged use of a drug may produce withdrawal symptoms on cessation of use.

10. High relapse rate. Many drug users quit several times before finally achieving permanent abstinence.[32]

The clear medical facts reveal the comprehensive effects alcohol abuse has on the human body. These effects range through the physical, cognitive, emotional, and spiritual domains of human existence. Physically, alcohol misuse negatively impacts and damages all organs in the human body, including the brain. Brain damage due to alcohol misuse has been plainly observed and documented, leading to cognitive impairment. For example, through the use of Single Photon Emission Computed Tomography (SPECT scans), Dr. Daniel G. Amen makes the following observations:

There is quite a bit of scientific literature about the harmful physiological effects of alcohol and drug abuse on the brain, SPECT scans of substance abusers have demonstrated a number of abnormalities in brain areas known to be involved in behavior, such as the frontal and temporal lobes...the most common

---

31 This is called "associations." Also known as "triggers," I tell my patients that persons, places, events, or things historically associated with alcohol use create cravings. The "mother of all triggers" is Super Bowl Weekend; a long weekend, football game, social gatherings, and a mood of celebration and euphoria.

32 H. Thomas Milhorn, *Drug and Alcohol Abuse: The Authoritative Guide for Parents, Teachers, and Counselors* (New York: Plenum Press, 1996), 19-20.

similarity is that the brain has an overall toxic look to it; the SPECT studies look less active, more shriveled, less healthy overall and have a "scalloping effect," a wavy, rough sea-like appearance on the brain's surface. This pattern is also seen in patients who have been exposed to toxic fumes or have had oxygen deprivation. Normal brain patterns, on the other hand, show smooth activity across the cortical surface.[33]

The following SPECT scans reflect the brain of an alcohol abuser. The negative eff cts of alcohol misuse over time causes comprehensive brain degeneration, affecting the limbic system, normal neuron and synapse malfunction, and neurotransmitter failure, directly damaging six critical brain neurotransmitters.[34]

BRAIN SCANS OF ALCOHOL ABUSERS

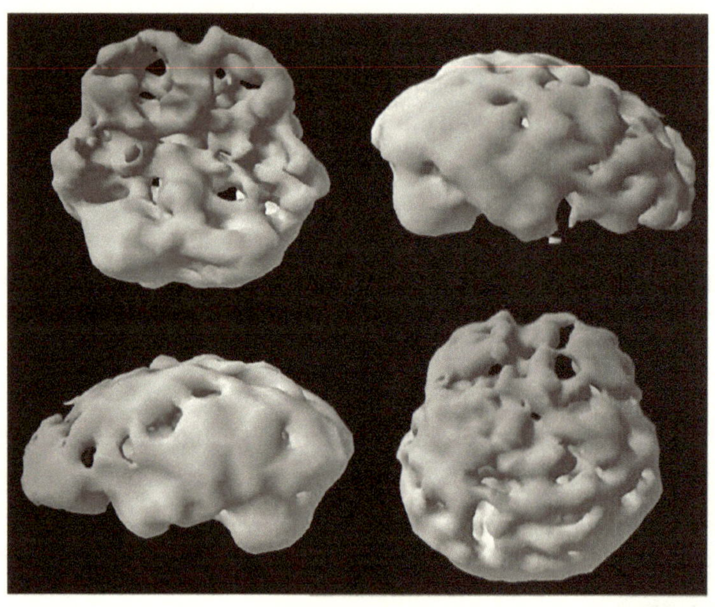

---

33 Daniel G. Amen, "Looking at the Brain Changes Everything," last modified November 1, 2016, accessed June 15, 2018. www.amenclinics.com.

34 Thomas Milhorn, *Drug and Alcohol Abuse: The Authoritative Guide for Parents, Teachers, and Counselors* (New York: Plenum Press, 1996), 21-25.

SPECT surface scans of the brain of a fifty-six-year-old man with daily use of three-four drinks but NOT an alcoholic. L to R, scans show brain from the bottom, right side, left side, and top down. The image in the bottom right corner (top down) compares to the image above–a top down view of a healthy brain. (Courtesy Amen Clinics, www.amenclinics.com)

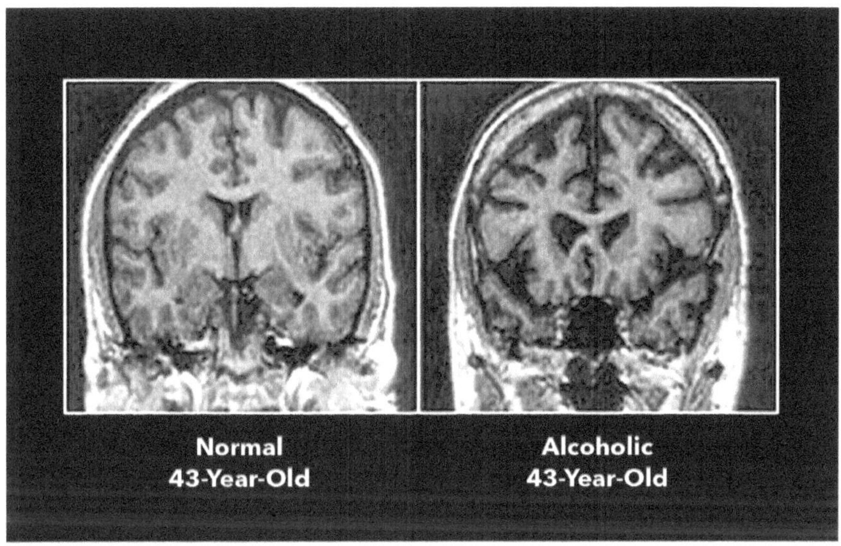

SPECT surface scans comparing the brains of a normal forty-three-year-old with that of an alcoholic forty-three-year-old. (Courtesy BRAINPICTURES. org, http:// brainpictures.org/p/37/alcoholic-brain/picture-37)

Brain structure and function involves literally billions of cells with trillions of interconnected chemical and electrical messages, stimulating, controlling, monitoring, and managing all bodily functions, including sleep patterns, involuntary nervous system reactions, and sensory input and interpretation.[35] Other physiologic functions and cognitive processes negatively impacted by alcohol misuse include judgment, fine motor

---

35 *National Geographic*, "Your Brain: 100 Things You Never Knew" (Washington, DC: *National Geographic*, 2018).

coordination, reflexes, voluntary responses to stimulation, sensation, breathing, and heart function.[36]

Spiritually, alcohol abuse is clearly addressed in the Bible as abhorrently sinful behavior. This sinful behavior creates spiritual poverty, pushing the alcohol abuser increasingly further away from a rich, personal relationship with Christ, surrendering the ability to experience the effects of the abundant life. Shaw's somber words reflect the role sin and self-centeredness play in alcohol-use disorders:

> Chemical addiction problems and excessive substance abuse really have two biblical names; one is a general name and the other more specific. In general, "idolatry" is the proper biblical name for substance abuse problems, whether you consider yourself a drunkard, binge drinker, drug addict, substance abuser, or whatever name you wish to call it. The problem is biblically labeled as the sin of idolatry and it is a heart problem from within one's sinful nature…the substance abuser seeks to please himself with his "god of choice" above pleasing God. The excessive user of alcohol and drugs is his own god; he is actively serving and pleasing the god of self by using drugs and alcohol. Ask yourself; "Am I serving God right now or seeking to please myself?"[37]

Over time, the medically and scientifically observed causes, effects, and progress of alcohol-use disorders have advanced in organization and systematization. The overarching "gold standard" in the medical community regarding alcohol misuse is, and has been, the *Diagnostic and Statistical Manual of Mental Disorders*, currently in its fifth edition (DSM-5).[38] The DSM-5 serves as the primary reference for alcohol misuse assessments, providing a comprehensive set of diagnostic criteria that provide a rich definition of mild, moderate, and severe alcohol-use

---

36 Cynthia Kuhn et al., Buzzed: *The Straight Facts About the Most Used and Abused Drugs from Alcohol to Ecstasy* (New York: Norton & Company, 2008), 39-47.

37 Mark E. Shaw, *The Heart of Addiction: A Biblical Perspective* (Bemidji, MN: FOCUS Publishing, 2008), viii-ix.

38 *Diagnostic and Statistical Manual of Mental Disorders*, 5th ed. (Arlington, VA: American Psychiatric Association, 2013).

disorders, establishing a quantifiable definition of what "moderation" looks like; generally, three or less standard drinks (12 ounces of beer; 1.5 ounces of liquor; or 5 ounces of wine) in one day designate the boundary between low-risk and high-risk drinking. For some time now, researchers have articulated the need for a quantifiable guideline that creates a line of demarcation between low-risk and high-risk alcohol use, highlighting the difference between alcohol use and abuse.[39]

Hundreds of research studies have been conducted over the past five decades, resulting in the "0-1-2-3-14 formula" for low-risk alcohol use.[40] This formula presents the alcohol user with an objective guideline for low-risk alcohol use as follows: zero use to ensure no-risk; no more than one standard drink an hour, *and* no more than two standard drinks in a sitting, *and* no more than three standard drinks in one day; finally, no more than fourteen standard drinks in one week. According to Dougherty and O'Brien, "There is substantial research to specify low-risk amounts for alcohol. Researchers from around the world have published over 200 scientific studies that can help us determine how many standard drinks would be low risk… (indicating) the quantities and frequencies of drinking that create risk for health or impairment problems."[41] This cumulative research has also led to the development of "colored stages of addiction" (Green-Yellow-Orange-Red), indicating increasing and definable risk levels of alcohol use and abuse.[42]

The list below provides a summary of the eleven specific DSM-5 diagnostic criteria for alcohol-use disorders:

1. Alcohol is often taken in larger amounts or over a longer period than was intended.
2. There is a persistent desire or unsuccessful efforts to cut down or control alcohol use.
3. A great deal of time is spent in activities necessary to obtain alcohol, use alcohol, or recover from its effects.

---

39 Cynthia Kuhn et al., Buzzed: *The Straight Facts About the Most Used and Abused Drugs from Alcohol to Ecstasy* (New York: Norton & Company, 2008), 47.
40 Ray Dougherty and Terry O'Bryan, *Prime for Life: Instructor Manual*, Version 9 (Lexington, KY: Prevention Research Institute, 2015), 64-71.
41 Ibid, 64.
42 Ibid, 83-121.

4. Craving, or a strong desire or urge to use alcohol.

5. Recurrent alcohol use resulting in a failure to fulfill major role obligations at work, school, or home.

6. Continued alcohol use despite having persistent or recurrent social or interpersonal problems caused or exacerbated by the effects of alcohol.

7. Important social, occupational, or recreational activities are given up or reduced because of alcohol use.

8. Recurrent alcohol use in situations in which it is physically hazardous.

9. Alcohol use is continued despite knowledge of having a persistent or recurrent physical or psychological problem that is likely to have been caused or exacerbated by alcohol.

10. Tolerance, as defined by either of the following: (a) A need for markedly increased amounts of alcohol to achieve intoxication or desired effect (b) A markedly diminished effect with continued use of the same amount of alcohol.

11. Withdrawal, as manifested by either of the following: (a) The characteristic withdrawal syndrome for alcohol (refer to criteria A and B of the criteria set for alcohol withdrawal) (b) Alcohol (or a closely related substance, such as a benzodiazepine) is taken to relieve or avoid withdrawal symptoms.[43]

In combination with other corollary diagnostic instruments (e.g., "Alcohol Use Disorder Identification Test" [AUDIT], "CAGE;" "Basic Addiction Measure" [BAM]; and self-reported intoxication and alcohol use over the past 12 months), the DSM-5 diagnosticcriteria setdiscrete boundariesinidentifying alcohol-related disorders, resulting in any one of the following three diagnoses: Alcohol Use Disorder-Mild (AUD -Mild); Alcohol Use Disorder-Moderate (AUD-Moderate); and Alcohol Use Disorder-Severe (AUD-Severe).[44]

Further systemization of alcohol misuse involves the level of medical treatment an individual should receive if struggling with an alcohol-use disorder. The clear, repeated, and expected effects of alcohol misuse

---

43 *Diagnostic and Statistical Manual of Mental Disorders,* 5th ed. (Arlington, VA: American Psychiatric Association, 2013), 490-491.

44 Ibid., 490-503.

have been documented by the research and medical communities.[45] This information (general revelation) is crucial, providing evidence-based support to making spiritually mature decisions regarding alcohol use.

Just like the diagnostic criteria for alcohol use disorders have been systematized, so have the treatment protocols for individuals suffering from alcohol use disorders. These treatment protocols include psychoeducation, individual therapy, group therapy, pharmacotherapy, electroconvulsive shock treatment (ECT), and various forms of recovery groups. Levels of treatment ranges from outpatient, intensive outpatient, and inpatient treatment programs. The American Society of Addiction Medicine (ASAM) operationalized a classification system designed to give functional guidance to the process of addiction treatment.[46] This functional guidance is designed to provide a multidimensional assessment, clinically driven treatment protocol, with variable length of service, over a continuum of care.[47]

Self-help groups serve as an additional resource for personal recovery. Three of these groups are highlighted in the following section.

The first organized attempt to provide hope for those overwhelmed by their misuse of alcohol occurred in 1935 with the founding of the "Grandfather of Recovery Programs," Alcoholics Anonymous (AA).[48].[48] Rooted and grounded in a 12-step program, AA provides a weekly (or in some cases, daily) support group that intentionally works through these 12 steps, summarized below:

1. We admitted we were powerless over alcohol—that our lives had become unmanageable. (Many alcoholics deny they cannot control their alcohol use. Once they honestly admit they are unable to stop on their own, the recovery process can begin.)
2. Came to believe that a power greater than ourselves could restore us to sanity. (While this step is not uniquely Christian, the existence and efficacy of a higher power is essential to recovery.)

---

45 R. H. Combs and William A. Howatt, *The Addiction Counselor's Desk Reference* (Hoboken, NJ: John Wiley & Sons, 2005), 4-6.

46 D. Mee-Lee, et al.

47 Ibid, 1.

48 Alcoholics Anonymous, *Twelve Steps and Twelve Traditions* (New York, Alcoholics Anonymous World Services, Inc., 1981),

3. Made a decision to turn our will and our lives over to the care of God as we understood Him. (For this step, the alcoholic consciously decides to turn themselves over to their higher power.)

4. Made a searching and fearless moral inventory of ourselves. (This is certain to be an uncomfortable, but necessary step leading to self-examination. Identifying areas of past regret, guilt, anger, or humiliation is important.)

5. Admitted to God, to ourselves, and to another human being the exact nature of our wrongs. (This step involves admitting to past poor behavior.)

6. Were entirely ready to have God remove all these defects of character.

7. Humbly asked Him to remove our shortcomings. (This step focuses the individual on humility and accountability.)

8. Made a list of all persons we had harmed and became willing to make amends to them all.

9. Made direct amends to such people wherever possible, except when to do so would injure them or others.

10. Continued to take personal inventory and when we were wrong promptly admitted it. (This step involves self-monitoring of negative behavior and attitudes.

11. Sought through prayer and meditation to improve our conscious contact with God, as we understood Him, praying only for knowledge of His will for us and the power to carry that out.

12. Having had a spiritual awakening as the result of these steps, we tried to carry this message to alcoholics, and to practice these principles in all our affairs. (This step encourages members to serve others who may be facing the same challenges.)[49]

Next, biblically based recovery programs have also emerged. Celebrate Recovery (CR) is the most recent, and most popular, recovery program, that developed out of "The Purpose Driven Life" movement.[50] Celebrate Recovery offers a powerful, spiritually based discipleship program as an

---

49 Alcoholics Anonymous, *Twelve Steps and Twelve Traditions* (New York, Alcoholics Anonymous World Services, Inc., 1981), 14.

50 Rick Warren, *The Purpose Driven Life: What on Earth Am I Here For?* (Grand Rapids, MI: Zondervan, 2002).

extension of the following eight specific Bible-focused steps based on the Beatitudes, and using the acronym RECOVERY:[51]

1. **R**ealize I'm not God; I admit that I am powerless to control my tendency to do the wrong thing and that my life is unmanageable. "Happy are those who know that they are spiritually poor" (Matthew 5:3 TEV).

2. **E**arnestly believe that God exists, that I matter to Him and that He has the power to help me recover. "Happy are those who mourn, for they shall be comforted" (Matthew 5:4 TEV, NIV).

3. **C**onsciously choose to commit all my life and will to Christ's care and control. "Happy are the meek" (Matthew 5:5 TEV).

4. **O**penly examine and confess my faults to myself, to God, and to someone I trust. "Happy are the pure in heart " (Matthew 5:8 TEV).

5. **V**oluntarily submit to any and all changes God wants to make in my life and humbly ask Him to remove my character defects. "Happy are those whose greatest desire is to do what God requires" (Matthew 5:6 TEV).

6. **E**valuate all my relationships. Offer forgiveness to those who have hurt me and make amends for harm I've done to others when possible, except when to do so would harm them or others. "Happy are the merciful" (Matthew 5:7 TEV); "Happy are the peacemakers" (Matthew 5:9 TEV).

7. **R**eserve a daily time with God for self-examination, Bible reading, and prayer in order to know God and His will for my life and to gain the power to follow His will.

8. **Y**ield myself to God to be used to bring this Good News to others, both by my example and my words. "Happy are those who are persecuted because they do what God requires" (Matthew 5:10 TEV).

---

51 John Baker, Johnny Baker, and Mac Owen, *Celebrate Recovery: 365 Daily Devotional: Healing from Hurts, Habits, and Hang-Ups* (Grand Rapids, MI: Zondervan, 2015).

The foundational element of spirituality within these recovery programs has been present since the beginning,[52] progressively moving from a generally Christian-based philosophy to a "spiritual living" concept,[53] and finally to a biblically based recovery paradigm.[54]

Additionally, biblically based relapse prevention programs have also emerged,[55] some with specific programs,[56] and relapse prevention strategies in workbook format.[57] Support and spiritual growth are also provided for those in recovery in the form of daily compendiums of thoughts for the day[58] and biblically based daily devotionals.[59]

Finally, for atheists, agnostics, and those not interested in spirituality, there exists "non-spiritual" programs like Rational Recovery.[60]

Connecting the Dots

"Spiritual Maturity, Alcohol Use Decisions, and Living the Abundant Life"

The impact of spiritual maturity on decisions regarding alcohol use is widely viewed as a protective factor preventing abuse and enhancing recovery. Even secular researchers and clinicians recognize the protective impact of spiritual maturity.[61] According to Vallant,

---

52 Alcoholics Anonymous, *Twelve Steps and Twelve Traditions* (New York: Alcoholics Anonymous World Services, Inc., 1981).

53 Rami Shapiro, *Recovery: The Sacred Art* (Woodstock, VT: Skylight Paths, 2013).

54 Friends in Recovery, *The Twelve Steps for Christians Based on Biblical Teachings* (Scotts Valley, CA: RPI Publishing, Inc, 2012).

55 Terence T. Gorski, *Passages Through Recovery: An Action Plan for Preventing Relapse* (Center City, MN: Hazleden1989).

56 Larry Skrant, *Addicts of the Cross: A Christian 9-Step Program Big Book* (Abbotsford, WI: Anecko Press, 2016).

57 Mark E. Shaw, *Relapse Biblical Prevention Strategies* (n.c.: Focus Publishing, Inc, 2011).

58 Alcoholics Anonymous World Services, *Just for Today* (Van Nuys, CA: AA World Services, 1991).

59 John Baker, et al., *Celebrate Recovery 365 Daily Devotional: Healing from Hurts, Habits, and Hang-Ups* (Grand Rapids, MI: Baker Book House, 2013).

60 Jack Trimpey, "Rational Recovery," accessed June 15, 2018. https://www.the-alcoholism-guide.org/rational-recovery.html.

61 Secular researchers and clinicians generally refer to spiritual maturity as "spirituality" or "religion," viewing it as a "protective factor."

...religion, in ways that we appreciate but do not understand, provides forgiveness of sins and relief from guilt. Unlike many intractable habits that others find merely annoying, alcoholism inflicts enormous pain and injury on those around the alcoholic. As a result the alcoholic, already demoralized by his inability to stop drinking, experiences almost insurmountable guilt from the torture he has inflicted on others. In such an instance, absolution becomes an important part of the healing process.[62]

The biblical concept of Christian spiritual maturity is like a multi-faceted diamond whose various aspects all encompass the beauty of the whole. In the same way, spiritual maturity possesses many wide-ranging biblical principles, practices, and evidences that facilitate health and provide wisdom regarding alcohol use. At the foundation of spiritual maturity lies the concept of spiritual growth, the process by which spiritual maturity is achieved. May describes the process of spiritual growth with the following words:

Authentic spiritual wholeness, by its very nature, is open-ended. It is always in the *process* of becoming, always incomplete. Thus we ourselves must also be always incomplete. If it were otherwise, we could never exercise our God-given right to participate in ongoing creation. The course of our lives is precisely as Saint Augustine indicated: our hearts will never rest nor are they meant to rest, until they rest in God. This precious restlessness is mediated by and manifested through our physical being, through the combined minute struggling of the cells of our brains and bodies as they seek harmony and balance in their endless adjustment to circumstances.[63]

An abundance of wide-ranging biblical passages describe this theme of growth in the Christian life (see Appendix 3). Peter commands believers to "grow in the grace and knowledge of the Lord Jesus Christ" (Second Peter 3:18). The lexical meaning of the word "grow" in this verse references consistent, active, progressive growth. Translated from the Greek αὐξανετε δε (*auxanete*

---

62 George E. Vallant, *The Natural History of Alcoholism Revisited* (London: Harvard University Press, 1995), 243.

63 Gerald G. May, *Addiction & Grace* (New York: Harper Collins Publisher, 1988), 181.

de), this present active imperative of αὐξάνω [*auxanō*], literally means "but keep on growing."[64] Chafer and Walvoord note, "Experiential sanctification is related to Christian growth. Christians are immature in wisdom, knowledge, experience, and grace. In all these things they are appointed to grow, and their growth should be manifest."[65] Clearly, the concept of spiritual growth and maturity in the Christian life is a *progressive* process and foundational to the process of decision-making regarding the use of alcohol.

The apostle Paul presents the visage of spiritual growth in the phrase "to a mature man, to the measure of the stature which belongs to the fullness of Christ" in his classic definition of the goal of spiritual growth for the Christian, in Ephesians 4:11-13:

> And He gave some as apostles, and some *as* prophets, and some *as* evangelists, and some as pastors and teachers, for the equipping of the saints for the work of service, to the building up of the body of Christ; until we all attain to the unity of the faith, and of the knowledge of the Son of God, to a mature man, to the measure of the stature which belongs to the fullness of Christ (NASB).

The writer of the book of Hebrews speaks metaphorically in using "milk" to refer to spiritual immaturity and stunted growth, and "solid food" as reflective of spiritual maturity, with these cutting words:

> There is much more we would like to say about this, but it is difficult to explain, especially since you are spiritually dull and don't seem to listen. You have been believers so long now that you ought to be teaching others. Instead, you need someone to teach you again the basic things about God's word. You are like babies who need milk and cannot eat solid food. For someone who lives on milk is still an infant and doesn't know how to do what is right. Solid food is for those who are mature, who through training have the skill to recognize the difference between right and wrong (Hebrews 5:11-14).

---

64 A. T. Robertson, *Word Pictures in the New Testament*, Second Peter 3:18 (Nashville, TN: Broadman Press, 1933).

65 Lewis Sperry Chafer and John F. Walvoord, *Major Bible Themes* (Grand Rapids, MI: Zondervan, 1974), 209.

In the same vein, Paul laments the lack of spiritual growth among the Christians at the church in Corinth with this polemic: "Dear brothers and sisters, when I was with you I couldn't talk to you as I would to spiritual people. I had to talk as though you belonged to this world or as though you were infants in Christ. I had to feed you with milk, not with solid food, because you weren't ready for anything stronger. And you still aren't ready" (First Corinthians 3:1-2). Stunted spiritual growth and immaturity has been an overarching challenge for Christians throughout history. Regarding this challenge to the contemporary church, Robertson laments, "Alas, what a commentary on modern Christians."[66]

The fullness of Scripture presents a comprehensive picture of the meaning and criticality of Christian spiritual growth as the catalyzing principle behind spiritual maturity. Lexically, metaphorically, and imperatively, spiritual maturity is elevated as the intentional lifetime goal for the Christian. Chappell connects spiritual maturity to personal holiness, a pivotal consideration motivating decisions regarding alcohol use. He states, "God requires holiness not just in status but in life (Second Corinthians 6:14-18). He calls His people to live and *grow* in ways that honor Him and bless others (Romans 12:1-2; Ephesians 5:1-2; Second Peter 3:18)" (italics mine).[67]

The process of spiritual maturity is not only progressive but also repetitive, leading to comprehensive, personal transformation. In describing their view of the twelve steps of addiction recovery from alcohol misuse, Minirth, et al., give the following insight:

An element of enormous importance now is *repetition*, practicing again and again, in total submission to the will of Christ, the implementing of *new*, healthier thought processes, feelings, and behaviors. These are the building blocks for the addict's new lifestyle of responsible, drug-free living. Addicts must learn to face and admit on a daily basis.[68]

---

66 A. T. Robertson, *Word Pictures in the New Testament* (Nashville, TN: Broadman Press, 1933), notes on Hebrews 5:12.

67 Bryan Chappell, "Grace," in *Systematic Theology Study Bible* (Wheaton, IL: Crossway, 2017), 1702.

68 Frank Minirth, et al., eds., *Taking Control* (Grand Rapids, MI: Baker Book House, 1988), 112-113.

Spiritual growth specifically and discretely reinforces the Christian's union with Christ and "frees us to make good decisions about our lives."[69]

Understanding that Leads to Wise Living

"Psychoeducation " is one of those technical, six-syllable words that simply means education intended to lead to cognitive, behavioral, and spiritual change. According to Griffiths, psychoeducation refers to "…a range of individual, family, and group interventions that are focused on educating participants about a significant challenge in living, helping participants develop social and resource supports in managing the challenge, and developing coping skills to deal with the challenge."[70]

This book focuses on cognitive, behavioral, and spiritual domains in order to facilitate spiritually mature decisions regarding alcohol use. Psychoeducation serves as the tip of the theoretical spear, applying specific and tailored information to a specific group of participants with a demonstrated interest in Christian spiritual maturity and its impact on their alcohol-use decisions.

Psychoeducation wears two functional hats. On one hand, psychoeducation is rooted and grounded in the most current, evidence-based research regarding the development, progress, and treatment of alcohol-use disorders.[71] On the other hand, psychoeducation then takes this information, packages, and presents it in the most strategic way.[72] The ultimate goal of these twin functions is to catalyze positive, life-changing, functional learning, known in the addition treatment community as recovery.[73]

69　Kevin O'Brien, *The Ignatian Adventure* (Chicago: Loyola Press, 2011), 14.

70　C. A. Griffiths, "The Theories, Mechanisms, Benefits, and Practical Delivery of Psychosocial Educational Interventions for People with Mental Health Disorders." *International Journal of Psychosocial Rehabilitation*, 11 (1) (2006): 3.

71　P. M. G. Emmelkamp and E. Vedel, *Evidence-Based Treatment for Alcohol and Drug Abuse: A Practitioner's Guide to Theory, Methods, and Practice* (New York: Routledge. 2006).

72　T. A. La Salvia, "Enhancing Addiction Treatment Through Psychoeducational Groups," *Journal of Substance Abuse Treatment*, September-October, Vol. 10 (1993), 439-444.

73　C. A. Griffiths. "The Theories, Mechanisms, Benefits, and Practical Delivery of Psychosocial Educational Interventions for People with Mental Health Disorders." *International Journal of Psychosocial Rehabilitation, 11*(1), 21-28 (2006), 21-28.

Psychoeducation attempts to energize learning, motivation, and recovery from addictions in two specific ways: prevention and intervention.[74] This book recognizes both processes of prevention and intervention: providing biblical and evidence-based psychoeducation to facilitate spiritual growth, in order to prevent problems surrounding alcohol-use decisions and creating possible alcohol-use-related intervention opportunities for ourselves, as well as the lives of others, such as family members, friends, or co-workers.

The purpose of this section is to suggest an approach to psychoeducation and decisions regarding alcohol use that is both balanced and biblical. This is especially important for Christianity in general, and, particularly, individual Christians who may be suffering from addiction. This section does not claim to portray a final solution to the biblical basis of psychoeducation, but to articulate a biblically centered and balanced view of addiction basics and the place of psychoeducation. From the biblical perspective, the process of psychoeducation can also be viewed as discipleship.

Historically, the causes of addiction have been expressed by a wide range of theoretical formulations and evidence-based observations. These theories include the Theory of Sin, the Disease Theory, the Genetics Theory, the Social-Learning Theory, and the Personality Theory.[75] The most recent evidence-based theory of addiction is the Neurological Disorder theory.[76]

From an integrative perspective, the most balanced approach is to view addiction as a combination of the above, co-occurring over time. All of these theories, generally, present aspects of addiction that should be considered uniquely, on a case-by-case basis, exclusive of the following two notable exceptions: the theory of Sin/Choice and the Disease/Neurological Disorder theories. The reason for this is clear: both theories present "universal truth" regarding the development and progress of alcohol-use disorders. This universal truth emerges out of evidence-based science and biblically based moral and spiritual truth.

---

74 I.. D. Yalom, *The Theory and Practice of Group Psychotherapy*, 5th ed. (New York: Basic Books, 2005).

75 Marc Lewis, *The Etiology of Desire: Why Addiction Is Not a Disease* (New York: PublicAffairs, 2016).

76 R. H. Coombs and W. A. Howatt, *The Addiction Counselor's Desk Reference* (Hoboken, NJ: John Wiley & Sons, 2005), 41-44.

The biblical reason for addiction begins with moral choice, but develops from there through an observable and predictable process, ultimately ending in the death of the alcohol abuser.[77] Regarding the moral and spiritual reason for addiction as reflected biblically, Minirth, et al. note: "While sin is certainly involved in becoming an alcohol or other drug *abuser* (the stepping-stone to becoming an addict), by the time one becomes an addict, choosing to abuse a drug is no longer a clear mental choice. Addiction is more a result of *former* sinful choices than of present ones."[78]

The biblical principle addressing alcohol abuse is clear and boils down directly to the heart of the matter. The following two primary passages are representative of the exhaustive biblical teaching surrounding the issue of alcohol abuse:

Proverbs 23:29-34: "Who has anguish? Who has sorrow? Who is always fighting? Who is always complaining? Who has unnecessary bruises? Who has bloodshot eyes? It is the one who spends long hours in the taverns, trying out new drinks. Don't gaze at the wine, seeing how red it is, how it sparkles in the cup, how smoothly it goes down. For in the end it bites like a poisonous snake; it stings like a viper. You will see hallucinations, and you will say crazy things. You will stagger like a sailor tossed at sea, clinging to a swaying mast. And you will say, 'They hit me, but I didn't feel it. I didn't even know it when they beat me up. When will I wake up, so I can look for another drink?'"

This proverb is one of 3,000 other proverbs and 1,005 songs written by King Solomon (First Kings 4:32), approximately 3,000 years ago. This passage represents an impressively accurate and conclusive definition of the destructive results of alcohol abuse and has been labeled "a case study of a drunkard."[79]Noted Old Testament linguist and theologian Bruce K.

77　D. G. D. Mee-Lee, et al., *ASAM Patient Placement Criteria for the Treatment of Substance-Related Disorders* (Chevy Chase, MD: American Society of Addiction Medicine, Inc., 2001).

78　Frank Minirth, et al., eds., *Taking Control* (Grand Rapids, MI: Baker Book House, 1988), 55.

79　Charles C. Ryrie, *The Ryrie Study Bible* (Chicago: Moody Press, 1978), note on Proverbs 23:29.

Waltke observes, "(In this passage, the main thought) underscores that the continued seeking is not an isolated occurrence. The passage describes more than a night's drinking and morning's hangover. It describes the increasingly degenerative effects, physical and mental, of the habitual drinker and the alcoholic (cf. John 8:34-36; First Corinthians 6:10-11)."[80]

Through the use of Hebrew poetic synthetic parallelism,[81] Solomon provides a comprehensive description of the risk associated with, and the disharmonious effects of drunkenness, summarized in the following exegetical list:

1. Drunkenness produces anguish and sorrow.
2. Drunkenness produces social hostility.
3. Drunkenness creates discontent.
4. Drunkenness contributes to physical injury.
5. Drunkenness produces physical discomfort and degeneration.
6. Drunkenness "bites like a poisonous snake, stings like a viper."
7. Drunkenness creates cognitive distortions and mental erosion.
8. Drunkenness destroys physical coordination.
9. Drunkenness erodes spiritual focus.
10. Drunkenness creates addiction.

The idea these verses establish is that there are specific, predictable cause-and-effect consequences to alcohol abuse as listed above. Regarding the grammatical purpose of the use of Hebrew parallelism, MacArthur notes: "One of the most common characteristics of Proverbs is the use of parallelism; that is, placing truths side-by-side so that the second statement expands, completes, defines, and emphasizes the first statement. Sometimes a logical conclusion is reached; at other times, a logical contrast is demonstrated."[82]

---

80 Bruce K. Waltke, *The Book of Proverbs: Chapters 15-31* (Grand Rapids, MI: William B. Eerdmans Publishing Company, 2005), 267.

81 Ibid., 263.

82 John MacArthur, *The MacArthur Bible Handbook: A Book-by-Book Exploration of God's Word* (Nashville: Thomas Nelson Inc, 2013), 167.

The warning evoked by this proverb regarding alcohol-use decisions is clear: vigilance must be consistently applied to decisions regarding the use of alcohol in order to ensure the "line of abuse" is not crossed.

Romans 13:13-14: "Because we belong to the day, we must live decent lives for all to see. *Don't participate in the darkness of wild parties and drunkenness*, or in sexual promiscuity and immoral living, or in quarreling and jealousy. Instead, clothe yourself with the presence of the Lord Jesus Christ. And don't let yourself think about ways to indulge your evil desires" (emphasis mine).

This central New Testament passage, which decries alcohol abuse, illustrates what I call the "Principle of Equivalent Sin." This principle weaves its way throughout the Bible, in order to drive home the pivotal spiritual principle that *any* sin separates us from God. This law mitigates against a "hierarchy of sins" (i.e., a spiritual paradigm we so quickly create in our minds that some sins are "more serious" than other sins). In this passage from Romans 13, the apostle Paul utilizes the "Principle of Equivalent Sin" by linking all sin in the following list summarized from this passage:

1. Indecent living
2. Darkness
3. Wild parties and drunkenness
4. Sexual promiscuity
5. Immoral living
6. Quarreling
7. Jealousy
8. Absence of the presence of Christ
9. Evil desires

The most important exegetical point that can be extracted from this passage is this: *There is no hierarchy of sin ... it all falls short of God's perfect standard of holiness.* Drunkenness (alcohol abuse) is characterized as sin that falls short of God's perfect standard. It is categorized with other sins that have traditionally been considered by Christians as "more serious sins." Even a perfunctory study of God's Word reveals this transcendent truth: *All have sinned and fallen short of the glory of God* (Romans 3:23).

Seen through the divine lens, all sin is a violation of God's plan and desire for the Christian life. Witmer notes, "Such actions and attitudes have no place in a Christian's life. He belongs to 'the light'; these deeds and thoughts belong to the darkness."[83]

Why does alcohol abuse not have a place in the Christian life? One central reason is the second coming of Christ and what He will find Christians doing when He *does* return. According to Boa and Kruidenier:

Paul told the Ephesians, "Let there be no sexual immorality, impurity, or greed among you. Such sins have no place among God's people. Obscene stories, foolish talk, and coarse jokes—these are not for you. Instead, let there be thankfulness to God" (Ephesians 5:3-4). Why? Because all of those things will be made visible on the day of our salvation. Better to come out of the darkness now and be found pure and holy when the light of the glory of God shines on all people at the end of this age. Light and darkness are incompatible in the spiritual realm just as they are in the physical realm. They cannot be in the same place (see First Thessalonians 5:5).[84]

Alcohol abuse is one of those deprecating sins. Mounce recounts the following story from Augustine's *Confessions*:

Our conduct is to be decent and honorable (v. 13). It must be acceptable in the open light of day. One example is Augustine. In his *Confessions,* he tells of his conversion to Christianity (viii.12). In a.d. 386, at a time when he was deeply moved by a desire to break from his old way of living, he sat weeping in the garden of a friend in Milan. Suddenly, he heard a child singing *Tolle, lege. Tolle, lege* ("Take up and read. Take up and read."). He picked up a scroll lying there, and his eyes fell on Romans 13:13-14: "Not

---

83 John A. Witmer, "Romans." In J. F. Walvoord and R. B. Zuck, eds., *The Bible Knowledge Commentary: An Exposition of the Scriptures,* Vol. 2 (Wheaton, IL: Victor Books, 1985), 491.

84 Kenneth Boa and William Kruidenier, *Romans,* Vol. 6 (Nashville, TN: Broadman & Holman, 2000), 401.

in orgies and drunkenness ..." Immediately his heart was flooded with a clear light, and the darkness of doubt vanished. No other theologian has made a greater contribution to the theology of the Western world and debauchery."

In John's Gospel we learn that people prefer darkness to light because their deeds are evil (John 3:19). Darkness hides, but light discloses. Evil flourishes in darkness because its perpetrators assume, although incorrectly, that what they are doing cannot be seen. The desire for darkness is itself an admission of the wrongness of the act. Along with the more socially repugnant acts of drunkenness and debauchery we find, rather unexpectedly, quarreling and jealousy. These too are acts of darkness. *Unfortunately, the church is considerably more tolerant toward such sins. Quarreling and jealousy, while not especially polite, are more acceptable than sexual immorality. This is not to make a case for immorality but to remind ourselves that Paul placed them together as deeds of darkness* (emphasis mine).[85]

The primary engine that drives the Christian life is a proper understanding of, commitment to, and application of spiritual maturity to the decisions of life. And it is spiritual maturity that will provide the necessary wisdom and guidance regarding the Christian's decisions related to alcohol use.

While there are many facets and components of Christian spiritual maturity, Tan presents a concise, yet insightful, list of seven major components of spiritual maturity summarized as follows:

1. Having a deep hunger or thirst for God (Psalm 42:1-2; Matthew 5:6).
2. Having a love for God based on personal knowledge of God resulting in worship of God and obedience to His good and perfect will (Matthew 22:17, 38; John 14:21, 23; Revelation 2:1-7).
3. Being fulled with the Holy Spirit and surrendering to God's deepening work of grace in our hearts and not yielding to the sinful nature or the flesh in us (Ephesisan 5: 18; Galatians 5:16; Romans 6:12-13).

---

85 Robert H. Mounce, *Romans*, Vol. 27 (Nashville: Broadman & Holman, 1995), 248.

4. Discovering and using the spiritual gifts given by the Holy Spirit for God's purposes and glory (Romans 12; First Corinthians 12; Ephesians 4; First Peter 4).

5. Developing biblical thinking and having a worldview that is consistent with God's eternal perspective as revealed in the Bible, His inspired Word (Romans 12:2; Philippians 4:8; Colossians 3:16; Second Timothy 3:16-17).

6. Being involved in spiritual warfare that requires the use of supernatural power and resources from God (First Corinthians 4:20; Ephesians 6:10-18).

7. Intentionally transforming into the image of Christ through all experiences daily (Philippians 3:10).[86]

This definitive list of the aspects of spiritual maturity transcend the intent of this book, but the primary principle remains: *spiritual growth is progressive, resulting in spiritual maturity, which, in turn, provides wisdom in decision-making regarding alcohol use.* Johnson calls this "the redemptive self," which provides the growth, wisdom, and hope for recovery. He notes:

As Christians believingly enter into this story, their identity, values, and relationships are becoming discretely transformed; meaning is gradually being made of their past, and hope for the future slowly emerges ... a transcendent break has been made between me and my past, and I am learning I don't have to repeat it, because Christ has given me new possibilities. The formation of this "redemptive self" may be particularly helpful for those who have lived chronically defeated lives due to highly debilitated personal agency, as seen in long-term addiction.[87]

A foundational, two-fold principle of Christian spiritual maturity and its influence in decisions regarding alcohol use is this: a growing spiritual relationship with God will provide me the *confidence* (Matthew 6:33) and

---

86 Siang-Yang Tan, *Counseling and Psychotherapy: A Christian Perspective* (Grand Rapids, MI: Baker Academic, 2011), 368-370.

87 Eric L. Johnson, *God & Soul Care: The Therapeutic Resources of the Christian Life* (Downers Grove, IL: IVP Academic, 2017), 380-381.

strength (Philippians 4:13) to make wise choices.[88] Calhoun asserts spiritual maturity results from practicing "Spiritual Disciplines." This involves understanding "rules for life" and "the rhythms of grace," both of which must revolve around a growing and deepening relationship of grace with God. The primary idea behind spiritual disciplines is *intentionality*. In order to experience success in all areas of our lives through the continuous application of God's wisdom to daily decisions, we must be actively involved in spiritual growth and the maturing process.[89]

Finally, some have asked, "How will I know if I am experiencing spiritual growth and maturity?" Great question. The answer? Just look in the mirror and note what you see. Biblically, the answer lies in the fruit my life is exhibiting. Paul talks about this in Galatians 5:19-24:

> *The acts of the flesh* are obvious: sexual immorality, impurity and debauchery; idolatry and witchcraft; hatred, discord, jealousy, fits of rage, selfish ambition, dissensions, factions and envy; *drunkenness*, orgies, and the like. I warn you, as I did before, that those who live like this will not inherit the kingdom of God. But *the fruit of the Spirit is love, joy, peace, forbearance, kindness, goodness, faithfulness, gentleness and self-control.* Against such things there is no law. Those who belong to Christ Jesus have crucified the flesh with its passions and desires (NIV, emphasis mine).

Drunkenness is clearly a fruit of the flesh (sin), while the fruit of the Spirit is equally distinct. We must regularly evaluate our spiritual maturity by looking in the mirror of God's Word. The principle is clear: a mirror is designed to portray reality, unless it is a distorted, carnival mirror.

This book uses psychoeducation in the twin realms of spiritual maturity and evidence regarding alcohol abuse to facilitate spiritually mature decisions regarding alcohol use, originally accomplished in a group setting.

---

88 June Hunt, *Counseling Through Your Bible Handbook* (Eugene, OR: Harvest House Publishers, 2008), 8.

89 Adele Ahlberg Calhoun, *Spiritual Disciplines Handbook: Practices that Transform Us* (Downers Grove, IL: IVP Books, 2015), 24-25.

Psychoeducation within a group setting has proven to be especially effective.[90] Biblically based psychoeducation groups have shown remarkable impact and are increasing in popularity.[91] Clinton and Ohlschlager state:

> ...human beings have three basic needs that can be dealt with most effectively in the context of a Christ-centered group: (1) the need to be, (2) the need to belong and to have goals, and (3) the need to do something with regard to these goals. A Christ-centered group can help members see the nature of God's love and forgiveness through the love and care of fellow group members as they bring their concerns to the Cross.[92]

The *progressive* nature of addiction is clear; initially the decision to use or abuse is a distinct cognitive, moral, and spiritual decision, primarily because the use of alcohol triggers the pleasure center of the brain.[93] However, as the disorder progresses, cognitive, moral, and spiritual decision-making becomes more cloudy and increasingly sabotaged by the escalating physical and neurological need to use. Lewis insightfully points out:

> One of the greatest blows to the current notion of addiction as a disease is the fact that behavioral addictions can be just as severe as substance addictions. The party line of NIDA, the AMA, and the American Society of Addiction Medicine remains what it has been for decades; addiction is primarily caused by substance abuse. But if that were so, why are addictions to porn, sex, Internet games, food, and gambling so ubiquitous? And why do "disorders" characterized by too much of many of the above show brain activation patterns that are nearly identical to those shown in

---

90 T. A. La Salvia, "Enhancing Addiction Treatment Th ough Psychoeducational Groups," *Journal of Substance Abuse Treatment*, September-October, Vol. 10 (1993).

91 E. L Worthington et al., "A Psychoeducational Intervention to Promote Forgiveness in Christians in the Philippines." *Journal of Mental Health Counseling* 32, no. 1 (2010): 75.

92 T. Clinton and G. Ohlschlager, *Competent Christian Counseling*, Vol. 1 (Colorado Springs, CO: The Waterbrook Press, 2012), 440-441.

93 E. M. Jellinek, *The Disease Concept of Alcoholism* (Mansfield Center, CT: Martino Publishing, 2010).

drug addiction (e.g., overactivation of the striatum when cues are present and anticipation is high, and deactivation of some prefrontal regions when indulgence takes the lead)?[94]

The point is this: regardless of the *reason* for addiction, *choice* still has a central role to play in the *process* of addiction.[95] The key presuppositional points behind these observations regarding alcohol-use disorders (AUD) and the moral decision-making process are reflective of two of the major addiction theories: the Choice Model and the Disease Model, The Choice Model emphasizes the fact that individual choice is the primary cause of addiction, while the Disease Model highlights the genetic, physiological, and cognitive *progressive* processes involved in the addiction process.[96]

Figure 1 (below) illustrates this progressive dynamic and the shift in influence from the moral decision-making process to the influence of the process of addiction:

Figure 1: Moral Decision-Making Power vs. Alcohol Influence

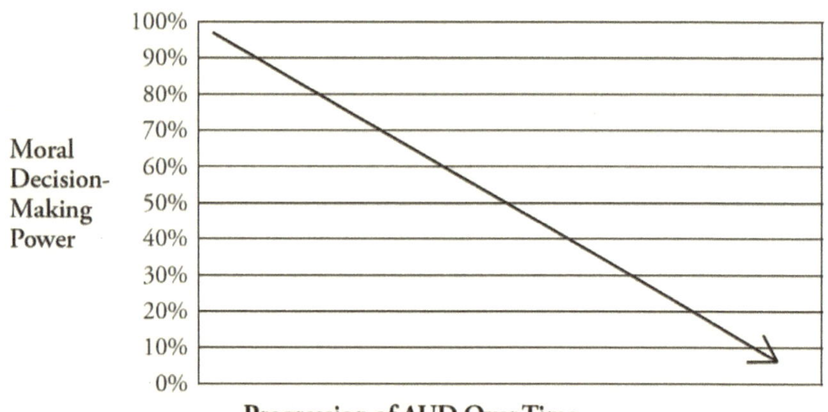

---

94 Marc Lewis, *The Biology of Desire: Why Addiction Is Not A Disease* (New York: P ublica Affairs, 2015), 165.

95 Darryl S. Inaba and William E. Cohen, *Uppers, Downers, All-Arounders: Physical and Mental Effects of Psychoactive Drugs* (Medford, OR: CNS Publications, 2011).

96 Tim Clinton and Eric Scalise, *Addictions and Recovery Counseling* (Grand Rapids, MI: Baker Books, 2013), 27.

According to the National Institute on Drug Abuse:

The initial decision to take drugs is typically voluntary. However, with continued use, a person's ability to exert self-control can become seriously impaired; this impairment in self-control is the hallmark of addiction. Brain imaging studies of people with addiction show physical changes in areas of the brain that are critical to judgment, decision making, learning and memory, and behavior control. Scientists believe that these changes alter the way the brain works and may help explain the compulsive and destructive behaviors of addiction.[97]

Welch labels this the dual nature of addiction, beginning as a choice and continuing as enslavement, as "voluntary slavery." He notes,

This enlarged perspective indicates that in sin, we are both hopelessly out of control and shrewdly calculating; victimized yet responsible. All sin is simultaneously pitiable slavery and over-rebelliousness or selfishness. This is a paradox to be sure, but one that is the very essence of all sinful habits. If you deny the out-of-control nature of all addictions, as some Christians have done, then you assume that everyone would have the power to change himself. Change would be easy… addiction is bondage to the rule of a substance, activity, or state of mind, which then becomes the center of life, defending itself from the truth so that even basic consequences don't bring repentance, and lead to further estrangement from God.[98]

The SPECT scans below again early illustrate the destructive progression of alcohol abuse on the brain. The devolving health and function of these critical organs in the human body present only a partial picture of the comprehensive damage done when alcohol is abused over time.[99]

---

97 National Institute on Drug Abuse, "Drug Abuse and Addiction." In *Journal of Brains and Behavior: The Science of Addiction,* July 2014. Accessed July 6, 2018. https://www.drugabuse.gov/publications/drugs-brains-behavior-science-addiction/drug-abuse-addiction.

98 Edward T. Welch, *Addictions-A Banquet in the Grave: Finding Hope in the Power of the Gospel* (Phillipsburg, NJ: P & R Publishing, 2001), 32, 35.

99 National Institute of Drug Abuse.

BRAIN SCANS OF ALCOHOL ABUSERS

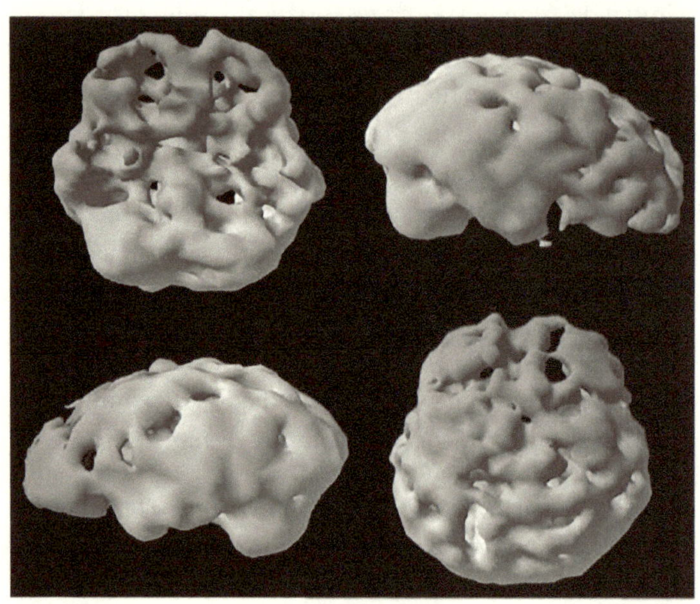

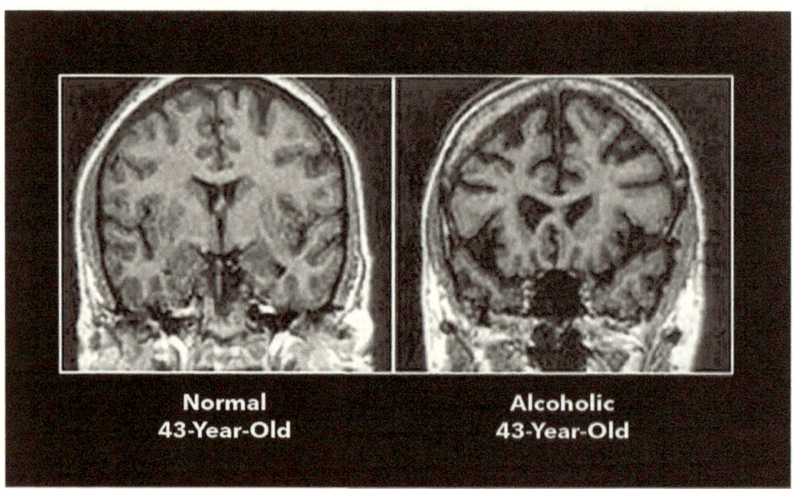

SPECT surface scans comparing the brains of a normal forty-three-year-old with that of an Alcoholic forty-three-year-old. (Courtesy BRAINPICTURES. org, http://brainpictures.org/p/37/alcoholic-brain/picture-37)

SPECT surface scans of the brain of a fifty-six-year-old man with daily use of three-four drinks but NOT an alcoholic. L to R, scans show brain from the bottom, right side, left side and top down. The image in the bottom right corner (top down) compares to the image above—a top down view of a healthy brain. (Courtesy Amen Clinics, www.amenclinics.com)

The character and impact of alcohol abuse is clear, both biblically and medically. This condition is predictable and definitive. Beginning with individual choice, it leads to slavery. It presents with clinically observable criteria, activates the reward center of the brain, and develops habits over time that comprehensively deteriorate all domains of life.[100]

A Sad Story

Sheri was a proven, mid-level manager within her organization, with twelve years of accumulated experience and notable successes. Due to her history of alcohol abuse, she appeared much older than her actual chronological age. She had been in treatment two times over the past four years, most recently thirty days of inpatient hospitalization due to withdrawal symptoms and her inability to manage her alcohol use. Upon discharge from the hospital, Sheri was now detoxed and had been sober for thirty days. As she began her outpatient treatment, she confidently proclaimed that she would be able to control her alcohol use moving forward. For the next ninety days of group and individual therapy, three-to-four recovery groups per week, and a powerful psychoeducation class, she was presented with the clear medical facts and warning regarding alcohol-use disorders. And, she was reminded daily that her medical diagnosis demanded she never use any alcohol for the rest of her life due to her clearly documented history of alcoholism. During her time in therapy, Sheri revealed she had come from a Christian home and attended church regularly growing up. She claimed to know Christ but "had fallen away from her faith over the past few years." While she did well in treatment, she was fired from her job due to her multiple alcohol-induced infractions. Additionally, her need for continuous treatment made her untrustworthy, undependable, and unable to perform her job.

---

100 *Diagnostic and Statistical Manual of Mental Disorders,* 5th edition (Washington, DC: American Psychiatric Publishing, 2013), 481.

Noticeable throughout her treatment was an absence of honesty on her part, failing to admit her abuse of alcohol had skewed her moral compass, degenerated her spiritual life and judgment, and made her powerless over the progressively degenerative effects of alcohol abuse. After her firing from her job, and before moving back home, she thanked all of her medical providers for the "excellent, life-changing treatment" she had received. Six months later those same medical providers received word about her progress: she died due to alcohol poisoning. Sadly, Sheri's failure to embrace principles of general and special revelation and live accordingly, proved to be deadly to her. Her two children were now orphans.

> **Critical Thought**
> *An honest evaluation of the fruit my life is bearing will act as a mirror and reveal the depth of my spiritual maturity.*

Questions for Further Thought

1. Review the list of ten character traits and stages of alcohol-use disorders on page 46-47. Is any of this currently true in your life?

2. If you currently use alcohol, has this had any negative impact on your life?

3. What have other people observed about your alcohol use, or have you ever felt guilty about it?

4. Has your alcohol use ever been the cause of job, relationship, or financial loss?

5. Review the list of alcohol-use disorder criteria on pp. 51-52. Are any true of your life?

3

One View of the Diamond

"Special Revelation: What Does the Bible Say About Alcohol Use?"

Understanding. The Bible provides all the special revelation God deems we need to know about experiencing the abundant life. This, however, does not happen by some kind of magical, spiritual osmosis. We need to be actively and intentionally studying the Bible in a systematized way as a normal and regular part of our lives. The Bible provides knowledge, understanding, and the resultant wisdom to make the many decisions demanded of our lives. Opinion or culture should be irrelevant; only a working knowledge of God's Word is acceptable for traveling the hazardous journey with which much of life challenges us. This includes the wisdom required for good decisions regarding alcohol use. Some have called this the "Way of Wisdom."

The Way of Wisdom

The Way of Wisdom has been a historical reference to the theological concept of the will of God. More specifically, it establishes a biblically based answer to the general concept of finding the will of God for my life.

"How do I find God's will?" has been a repeated mantra for innumerable Christians throughout history, but especially within the contemporary church. In a practical sense, this question creates a dilemma similar to attempting to nail jello to the wall. It elicits a second question: "How will I know when I have found God's will for my life?" Is there some kind of magic formula, special prayer, applicable devotional, or access to some sort of wise sage who can direct me in this endeavor? Should we cast lots, look for signs, study the stars (i.e., astrology), go to a fortune teller, have my palm read, or sit with a Tarot card reader? These are all activities in which some Christians have engaged or expressed sympathetic tolerance. Some have labeled the idea of finding God's will a "pagan notion."[1]

The traditional Christian view of the will of God is that there is a divinely ordained *individual will of God for every Christian*, implying there is a direction Christians must find for every decision we make in life. From what college to attend, what degree to earn, what city to live in, what house to buy, what neighborhood to live in, and what car to drive, are examples of decisions Christians who adhere to the traditional view of the will of God struggle with, hoping and praying they make the right decision *every* time a decision is needed. This only leads to anxiety and struggle. So, what *is* the will of God, where can it be found, and where can I find it for *every* decision in my life? Or could it be possible this traditional view of the will of God is not, after all, a biblical concept? Many would assert exactly that. So, what is the alternative? Those who teach a "nontraditional" view of the will of God (e.g., Friesen, Jones, MacArthur, Waltke), state simply that the Bible does not teach an individual will of God for every believer, but presents a framework of God's *moral* will, within which every Christian must live. This results in obedience to what God has revealed to us in His Word, while allowing us to apply principles of wisdom to every other decision we face in life. The church Fathers also subscribed to the importance of obedience. According to Young, "Obedience is the best ornament of the monk. He who has acquired it will be heard by God, and he will stand beside the crucified with confidence, for the crucified became obedient unto death (Philippians 2:8). Humility was to be achieved by the endurance of trials for the sake of Christ; that was the way to be blessed (Matthew 5:10ff)."[2]

The result of obedience to God's Word? Daily experiencing the freedom we have in Christ and the joy of that freedom in all of our non-moral decisions.

---

1   Bruce Waltke, *Finding the Will of God: A Pagan Notion?* (Gresham, OR: Veritas House Publishing, 1995), 23-74.

2   Frances M. Young, *Brokenness & Blessing: Toward a Biblical Spirituality* (Grand Rapids, MI: Baker Academic, 2007), 23.

In his classic work on the will of God, Friesen names this biblical approach to God's will for our lives the "way of wisdom," and proclaims:

> The Bible is fully sufficient to provide all guidance needed for a believer to know and do God's will …The expression *will of God* is used in the Bible in two ways. God's *sovereign will* is His secret plan that determines everything that happens in the universe. God's *moral will* consists of the revealed commands in the Bible that teach how people ought to believe and live.[3]

MacArthur asserts there are five things we are obligated to focus on regarding God's will: to be saved, sanctified, submissive to God's Word, filled with the Holy Spirit, and willing to suffer for the sake of Christ. He confidently states that if we focus on these five things, then we can do whatever we want to do.[4] This is part of what freedom in Christ means.

Jones comes to the same conclusion when he writes that the Bible must be our focus in knowing and following God's moral will for our life, which will result in confidence and clarity in ensuring a solid moral foundation that undergirds our decision-making process.[5]

Understanding the biblical basis of the will of God will establish a firm underpinning upon which I can build a life of solid, consistently healthy decision-making that honors God and obeys His Word. While the Bible never uses the phrase "find God's individual will for your life," it does provide a multitude of imperatival commands, exhortations, and warnings regarding knowing and obeying God's moral will. The repeated use of the imperative mood (command to do or not do something), throughout the Old and New Testaments, comprise the revealed will of God, around which Christian decision-making must revolve. Everything Christians need to know about the mind of God (His desire or will for my life), is contained in the Bible. The bottom line is this: to know, obey, apply, and follow biblical imperatives is to know the will of God for my life. It

---

3   Garry Friesen, *Decision Making and the Will of God* (Colorado Springs, CO: Multnomah Books, 2004), 41, 115-116.

4   John MacArthur, *Found: God's Will* (Colorado Springs, CO: David C. Cook, 2012), 67-68.

5   David W. Jones, *Knowing and Doing the Will of God* (Wake Forest, NC: Veritas Publications, 2017), 95-96.

is beyond dispute that biblically based guidance is synonymous with the revealed will of God. According to Challies:

> His revealed will is all those things he tells us to do in the Bible, and the things he has written upon our conscience. It is all those things he expects us to do to bring honor to him …God tells us how we may be sanctified and how we may be evermore conformed into the image of his Son. It is God's will for each of us that we grow in holiness, that we grow in our knowledge and love of God, and that we let the love of God shine through us.[6]

Within the pages of Scripture we are repeatedly reminded of the imperative to obey the revealed will of God, and exactly what that revealed will teaches us. Concise examples of this are listed below:

Romans 12:1-2: "And so, dear brothers and sisters, I plead with you to give your bodies to God because of all he has done for you. Let them be a living and holy sacrifice—the kind he will find acceptable. This is truly the way to worship him. Don't copy the behavior and customs of this world, but let God transform you into a new person by changing the way you think. Then you will learn to know God's will for you, which is good and pleasing and perfect".

Ephesians 5:17-18: "Therefore do not be foolish, but understand what the Lord's will is. Do not get drunk on wine, which leads to debauchery. Instead, be filled with the Spirit" (NIV).

First Thessalonians 4:3: "God's will is for you to be holy, so stay away from all sexual sin".

First Thessalonians 5:18: "Be thankful in all circumstances, for this is God's will for you who belong to Christ Jesus".

---

6   Tim Challies, *The Discipline of Spiritual Discernment* (Wheaton, IL: Crossway, 2007), 112.

Numerous other examples of God's will for us include all commands of commission and prohibition, as well as the Ten Commandments (see Appendix 3 for key passages regarding the will of God).

A proper understanding of the will of God is essential to establishing healthy decisions regarding alcohol use by Christians. Nature demonstrates the character of God and His design; the Bible encapsulates the definition of spiritual maturity, providing the wisdom and guidance necessary when making alcohol-use decisions. The following three biblically based principles are foundational to the application of spiritually mature alcohol-use decisions, and are reflective of the will of God for the Christian life.

You Are a Unique and Complex Design

A central biblical teaching regarding humanity is that God created us as complex, multi-dimensional beings. The creative act of God involving human beings clearly indicates comprehensive complexity of design (physical, cognitive, emotional, and spiritual).

Beginning at the biomolecular level, the fingerprint of God is clearly seen in its magnificence and complexity. According to Rana:

> So far, only a small portion of the splendor of life's chemistry has been captured in scientists' attempts to represent the structure, chemical interactions, and operational mechanisms of biochemical systems. Still, the magnificence of the cell's inner working is evident even in the "crude" images produced by biomolecular explorers ... Theists and atheists alike can see design in biological and biochemical systems. Even the well-known evolutionary biologist Richard Dawkins, an outspoken atheist, acknowledges that "biology is the study of complicated things that give the appearance of having been designed for a purpose."[7]

The introduction of alcohol into this complex, biomolecular formula creates potential divergence from normal function and high-risk dysfunction of these divinely designed systems. Hence, the impact of

---

7   Fazale Rana, *The Cell's Design: How Chemistry Reveals the Creator's Artistry* (Grand Rapids, MI: Baker Books, 2008), 16-17.

alcohol abuse affects all areas of life, making it a complex issue demanding multifaceted attention. The Bible clearly portrays human beings as complex and multidimensional. In his closing comments to the Thessalonian church, Paul wrote these words: "Now may the God of peace make you holy in every way and may your whole *spirit and soul and body* be kept blameless until our Lord Jesus Christ comes again" (First Thessalonians 5:23, emphasis mine). This clear distinction between spirit, soul, and body is evident throughout Scripture. Even a cursory review of the biblical evidence of the complex, multidimensional nature of human beings will reveal literally dozens of Bible verses referencing the various parts of the human design. According to Craig von Buseck:

> (In the Bible), mankind is distinct from all the rest of creation, including the animals; in man is three parts; body, soul, and spirit. Man is made up of physical material; the body, that can be seen and touched. But he is also made up of immaterial aspects, which are intangible. This includes the soul, spirit, intellect, will, emotions, conscience, and so forth. These immaterial characteristics exist beyond the physical lifespan of the human body and are therefore eternal. These immaterial aspects, the spirit, soul, heart, conscience, mind, and emotions, make up the whole personality.[8]

Laidlaw goes one step further by operationalizing each aspect of the various components of the human design stating, "…*spirit* represents the principle of life, *soul* the subject of life, and *heart* the organ of life; definitions, which will be found to apply accurately to all the three constituent lives which the human being can lead; (a) the physical, (b) the mental and moral, (c) the spiritual and religious."[9]

Other biblical occurrences of the multidimensional composition of human design include references to the various elements of this design (Genesis 2:7; Numbers 16:22; Psalm 139:13-14; Proverbs 4:23; Acts 23:1; Romans 12:1-2; and First Corinthians 2:14, 6:20), and the actual division

---

8   Craig von Buseck, "What Are the Three Parts of Man?" accessed on May 27, 2018. http://www1.cbn.com/questions/what-are-the-three-parts-of-man.

9   John Laidlaw, "The Immaterial Part of Man" in *Systematic Theology*, Vol. II, Lewis Sperry Chafer (Dallas: Dallas Seminary Press, 1974), 191-192.

between these various parts (Hebrews 4:12, reflecting that God is the only source of living words).[10] White addresses a very specific Old Testament reference to the various parts of human design, stating:

> The Hebrew word for the human being is *nepes*, which among its wide range of meaning connotes both flesh and soul as inseparable components of a person. A *nepes*, or person, is first of all a living being, animated by breath … a person is also composed of "soul," so the less concrete attributes also belong to the person. Appetites like desire, loathing, sorrow, joy, and love, and thought or mental activity all belong to the *nepes*.[11]

Norman Geisler brings a theological flavor to this discussion when he notes the following:

> Each individual human being is a unity of soul and body, having a spiritual dimension and physical dimension. Each partakes of the immaterial as well as the material, the angelic as well as the animal. As such, humans are unique; each is a psychosomatic unity, a blend of mind and matter. This unity of body and soul was evident from the very beginning, for the Lord God formed man from the dust of the ground (body) and breathed into his nostrils the breath of life (spirit), and the man became a human being (Genesis 2:7).[12]

The critical consideration at this point is understanding that alcohol, *when abused*, will damage and initiate a system-wide deterioration of human physiological functioning and balanced health. The catastrophic effects of alcohol abuse, over time, has been shown to comprehensively corrode brain functions, the gastrointestinal system, liver metabolic and filtering capabilities, hematological processes, cardiovascular functioning,

---

10   Norman Geisler, *Systematic Theology: God; Creation*, Vol. 2 (Minneapolis: Bethany House, 2003), 252.

11   Saidie Ann White, "Human Person." In *The Oxford Companion to the Bible*, Bruce M. Metzger and Michael D. Coogan, eds. (New York: Oxford University Press, 1993), 295.

12   Geisler, 452.

endocrine processes, metabolic activities, and a host of alcohol-induced disease and related disorders.[13] Spiritual degeneration, spiritual dwarfism, and habitual sin also result from alcohol abuse.[14]

Thus, the physical, cognitive, emotional, and spiritual aspects of our divine design must all be considered when evaluating the effects of alcohol on the user.

God Intends for You to Live Abundantly

The fact that God desires His children to live and experience the abundant life is beyond dispute. This fact is clearly taught by Jesus in John 10:10 when He declares, "The thief comes only to steal and kill and destroy; I came that they may have life and have it abundantly" (NASB). The central theme of this verse lies in the meaning and use of the word "abundantly." This English word reflects a rich, linguistic meaning, translated from the original Koine (common)[15] Greek word περισσὸν (*perisson*, literally meaning that they "may have abundance").[16] Other translations of περισσὸν include "in full" (NIV), "rich and satisfying" (NLT), and "in abundance" (HCSB). Louw and Nida comment, "Pertaining to a quantity so abundant as to be considerably more than what one would expect or anticipate; that which is more than more than enough, beyond the norm, abundantly, superfluous."[17] Wallace indicates περισσὸν refers to the manner in which Christians are to intentionally live out our lives.[18\]

The intended meaning of "abundantly" is a primary reference to the spiritual blessings of God in the life of the believer, coming through faith in Christ. There is no indication in Scripture, however, that this means

---

13 David E. Smith and Richard B. Seymour, *Clinician's Guide to Substance Abuse* (New York: McGraw-Hill Medical Publishing Division, 2001), 215-217.

14 Tim Clinton and Eric Scalise, *Addictions and Recovery Counseling* (Grand Rapids, MI: Baker Books, 2013), 23, 29.

15 Daniel B. Wallace, *Greek Grammar Beyond the Basics: An Exegetical Syntax of the New Testament* (Grand Rapids, MI: Zondervan Publishing House, 1995), 15-29.

16 M. R. Vincent, *Word Studies in the New Testament,* Vol. 2. (New York: Charles Scribner's Sons 1889), 192.

17 J. P. Louw and E. A. Nida. *Greek-English Lexicon of the New Testament: Based on Semantic Domains*, Vol. 1 (New York: United Bible Societies, 1996), 598–599.

18 Wallace, 293.

God will abundantly bless in the areas of material possessions or money. Known as "Prosperity Theology," and a distortion of God's intent for believers, creates a discussion beyond the intent of this book. Nevertheless, God *is* clearly the source of our essential material needs. Jesus taught in Matthew 6:31-33, "So don't worry about these things, saying, 'What will we eat? What will we drink? What will we wear?' These things dominate the thoughts of unbelievers, but your heavenly Father already knows all your needs. Seek the Kingdom of God above all else, and live righteously, and he will give you everything you need".

One of the most unambiguous teachings of the Bible, especially reflected in the discourses of Christ, is God's intent for Christians to experience the abundant life. It is a life that demonstrates the variegated grace, mercy, and blessings of God. From the perspective of neuroscience, intentionally living the abundant life serves as a protective factor regarding decisions about alcohol use. According to Jennings,

> Jesus came so that we might have life and have it more abundantly, here and now, as we anticipate the day that the mortal life puts on immortality (see John 10:10; First Corinthians 15:53). The abundant life is the life of love, which only occurs when we replace the twisted versions of God with truth, enabling God's love to flow through us to others. And it is in the prefrontal cortex that we comprehend truth, experience God's love, and altruistically love others.[19]

The abundant life is an earthly reflection of the divine, mirroring the overwhelming grace and riches of God that He desires to, and, in fact, has, poured out on those who know Christ personally, and who daily seek to live in obedience to Him. Christ declared in John 10:10 that this was the purpose of His first coming; that we might experience the abundant life. The New Testament brims with expressions of God's abundance, reflected especially with the synonymous use of the word "riches." The following verses from the NASB that impact this discussion summarize God's riches reflecting this abundance:

---

19   Timothy R. Jennings, *The God-Shaped Brain: How Changing Your View of God Transforms Your Life* (Downers Grove, IL: IVP Books, 2017), 43.

Romans 2:4: "Or do you think lightly of the riches of His kindness and tolerance and patience, not knowing that the kindness of God leads you to repentance?"

Romans 11:33-36: "Oh, the depth of the riches both of the wisdom and knowledge of God. How unsearchable are His judgments and unfathomable His ways."

Ephesians 2:4-5: "But God, being rich in mercy, because of His great love with which He loved us, even when we were dead in our transgressions, made us alive together with Christ (by grace you have been saved)."

Ephesians 2:7: "So that in the ages to come He might show the surpassing riches of His grace in kindness toward us in Christ Jesus."

Ephesians 3:8: "To me, the very least of all saints, this grace was given, to preach to the Gentiles the unfathomable riches of Christ."

Philippians 4:19: "And my God will supply all your needs according to His riches in glory in Christ Jesus."

Colossians 1:27: "… to whom God willed to make known what the riches of the glory of this mystery among the Gentiles is, which is Christ in you, the hope of glory."

Colossians 2:2-3: "… that their hearts may be encouraged, having been knit together in love, and attaining to all the wealth that comes from the full assurance of understanding, resulting in a true knowledge of God's mystery, that is, Christ Himself, in whom are hidden all the treasures of wisdom and knowledge".

So, how can alcohol abuse dilute God's riches? It cannot. God's riches and blessings stand on their own merit and reflect the character of God. Alcohol abuse can, however, create negative practical consequences in life, kidnapping the believer, and transporting him or her outside of God's desire and design for the Christian life. These consequences will be discussed later.

In light of biblical evidence, it is clear that God's desire for the believer is to live in a daily, practical sense, the abundant life in obedience to God's revealed Word. According to Kruse:

> The imagery is of a shepherd ensuring that his sheep are well cared for and contented. Jesus, the good shepherd, came into the world so that people might have (eternal) life, and have it to the full. To have eternal life is to know God through Jesus Christ (John 17:3). To have it to the full could refer either to enjoying the richness of life in relationship with God in the here and now or to resurrection to eternal life at the end of the age, or both.[20]

God's design of the abundant life for Christians, in many respects, surpasses the human imagination. The existence of the abundant life as *a way of life* that regulates the decisions Christians make, intentionally embracing the abundant life and all its direct and indirect protective factors, catapulting the decisions Christians make regarding alcohol use into the category of God-centered consideration that focuses on the eternal instead of "my here and now." The abundant life revolves around God's desire for living the Christian life versus indulging unhealthy and sinful human desires and appetites.

You Must Know and Obey God's Will

The concept of the will of God presents a wide-ranging discussion involving many different factors that orbit the character of God, nature of the church, teaching of the church Fathers, and the creeds and traditions embedded in Historical Theology.[21] The result of this kind of discussion would be a theological treatise far beyond the intent or scope of this book. For purposes of this book, the "will of God" is a direct reference to the Bible as the unique written Word of God. In the end, however, Bloesch asserts,

---

20 C. G. Kruse, *John: An Introduction and Commentary*, Vol. 4 (Downers Grove, IL: InterVarsity Press, 2003), 232.

21 Donald G. Bloesch, *Holy Scriptures: Revelation, Inspiration, & Interpretation* (Downers Grove, IL: InterVarsity Press, 1994).

The ultimate authority for faith is the living Word of God, the gospel of reconciliation and redemption, which is made known to the church but not delivered into the hand of the church. What the church passes on from one generation to another is teachings about the gospel ... the treasure of the gospel is transmitted not simply to the pope or to the bishops of the church but to the whole people of God, though it is imparted in such a way that it is never our possession but always our goal and hope. The apostle Paul declared, "Such a treasure is indeed ours, but it is carried by us in what are the vessels of clay to show that the power exceeding all else is God's and does not belong to ourselves" (Second Corinthians 4:7 GNC).[22]

Chafer adds, "God's will (the Bible) is the standard with which to measure all that is esteemed right in motive, design, and execution. ... There is nothing higher for man than to find and do the will of God."[23] Larson agrees when he notes:

The Bible originates with God. Claims of origins carry great significance because authority lives in the Creator. This is why people invest such Herculean efforts in trying to disprove God as the earth's Creator and in questioning the authenticity of the Bible. Admitting to God's authorship is an acceptance of his authority over every aspect of life. By stating that Scriptures are God-breathed, Paul established the Bible's claim as God's authoritative Word over all people.[24]

To know and obey God's will functions for the Christian like a road map functions for the traveler (Psalm 119). And where do we find God's will? There is only one source: the Bible (Second Timothy 3:16). The following table summarizes the biblical teaching regarding the character and authority of the Bible as the written Word and will of God:

---

22 Bloesch, 160-161.

23 Lewis Sperry Chafer, *Systematic Theology*, Vol. VII (Dallas: Dallas Seminary Press, 1974), 309.

24 K. Larson. *I & II Thessalonians, I & II Timothy, Titus, Philemon*, Vol. 9 (Nashville, TN: Broadman & Holman Publishers, 2000), 306.

Table 1: The Bible: God's Revealed Will

References	Function and Character
Psalm 19	Reflects the glory of God
Psalm 119:9	Provides spiritual cleansing
Psalm 119:1; Jeremiah 23:29	Like medicine to keep us from the sickness of sin
Psalm 119:105	Like a lamp to our feet so we can see our path
Isaiah 40:8	Eternal
Jeremiah 23:29	Breaks our pride
Luke 24:44; John 5:46; Acts 10:43	Points to Christ
John 17:17	Provides divine truth
Romans 15:4	Like a counselor that comforts us
Second Timothy 3:15	Is sacred Gives wisdom for salvation
Second Timothy 3:16	It is "God-breathed" Teaches Reproves Corrects Trains
Hebrews 4:12	Reveals motives of the heart
James 1:23-25	Like a mirror so we can see our true reflection
First Peter 1:23	Leads to spiritual rebirth and regeneration
First Peter 2:2; Matthew 4:4; Jeremiah 15:16	Provides spiritual nourishment
Second Peter 1:19	Like a forecaster that never fails us

Chafer provides the following powerful observations regarding the nature of God's Word and the absolute necessity for us to know and obey it: "Nothing could be more fundamental in the sphere of human knowledge than that God has caused His own Word to be written in a form which man can comprehend, and has preserved that Word through the ages of human history for the benefit of all men.... (It is) revelation from God, inspired by Him, with a life-imparting message, that must be rightly interpreted."[25]

As the living Word of God, the Bible is the wellspring of wisdom that leads to successful living in all areas of life; career, health, relationships, finances, and legal, resulting in spiritual and emotional growth. Wells notes, "This revealed Word defines for us how we should think about God, ourselves, our world, the church, and the future…references to sound teaching and doctrine, then, are a reminder to us that from such teaching strength, health, reversal of spiritual ills and deep paralysis, wholeness, vitality, and longevity results."[26]It is this divine wisdom that leads to the spiritual maturity necessary to make wise decisions regarding alcohol use.

Ultimately, biblical truth must be applied to the Christian life as a critical component of the spiritual disciplines, leading to increased spiritual intimacy with Christ on a daily basis. According to Calhoun, an age-old spiritual practice for Christians, resulting in deep spiritual intimacy, involved "praying the Scriptures." She observes:

> In the early centuries of the church, believers were taught to pray the Scriptures. Since the Bible is divinely inspired, they believed that praying Scripture deeply connected them to the mind and heart of God. Furthermore, as Scripture was repeatedly prayed it became memorized. This was a wonderful benefit for those who were illiterate. It also meant that memorized Scripture could lead them to pray at any hour of the day or night. Praying Scripture is a way of entering deeply into the text with a heart alert to a unique and personal word from God. Words and verses that catch our attention become invitations to be with God in prayer. When our prayers seem to be more about maintaining control and offering God our agenda for his stamp of approval, praying Scripture can return us to a simpler state of openness and attentiveness to God. We

---

25 Lewis Sperry Chafer, *Systematic Theology*, Vol. VII (Dallas: Dallas Seminary Press, 1974), 43-45.

26 David Wells, "What Is Doctrine and Why Is It Important?" In *Systematic Theology Study Bible* (Wheaton, IL: Crossway, 2017), 1619-1622.

lay aside our own agendas and open ourselves to the prayers given to us in the Bible.[27]

Knowledge and application of the Bible as the will of God for us will provide an invaluable directional azimuth for decisions regarding alcohol use. Despite opinions and debates to the contrary, the Bible is clear regarding what it teaches about alcohol use. The following biblical passages demonstrate that alcohol use, in and of itself, is not condemned.

Alcohol use

The question of alcohol use for the Christian has ignited many arguments and heated debates throughout the history of the church. However, contemporary scientific and medical research has created a body of evidence-based truth regarding the effects of alcohol on the human body, *especially* the abuse of alcohol. In combination with the biblically based truth expressed by the following verses, it is clear that alcohol is, in fact, allowed for Christians. As I have noted in other parts of this book, the pivotal issue is clearly *how much is too much.*

Genesis 14:18: "Then Melchizedek king of Salem brought out bread and wine. He was priest of God Most High" (NIV).

Genesis 27:25: "Then he said, 'My son, bring me some of your game to eat, so that I may give you my blessing.' Jacob brought it to him and he ate; and he brought some wine and he drank" (NIV).

Deuteronomy 14:24-26: "If the distance is so great for you that you are not able to bring *the tithe*, since the place where the Lord your God chooses to set His name is too far away from you when the Lord your God blesses you, then you shall exchange *it* for money, and bind the money in your hand and go to the place which the Lord your God chooses. You may spend the money for whatever your heart desires: for oxen, or sheep, or wine, or strong drink, or

27 Adele Ahlberg Calhoun, *Spiritual Disciplines Handbook: Practices that Transform Us* (Downers Grove, IL: IVP Books, 2015), 279.

whatever your heart desires; and there you shall eat in the presence of the Lord your God and rejoice, you and your household" (NASB).

Judges 9:13: "But the grapevine also refused, saying, 'Should I quit producing the wine that cheers both God and people, just to wave back and forth over the trees?'".

Psalm 104:14-15: "You cause grass to grow for the livestock and plants for people to use. You allow them to produce food from the earth, wine to make them glad, olive oil to soothe their skin, and bread to give them strength".

Ecclesiastes 8:15: "So I commend the enjoyment of life, because there is nothing better for a person under the sun than to eat and drink and be glad. Then joy will accompany them in their toil all the days of the life God has given them under the sun" (NIV).

Matthew 11:18-19: "For John came neither eating nor drinking, and they say, 'He has a demon.' The Son of Man came eating and drinking, and they say, 'Here is a glutton and a drunkard, a friend of tax collectors and sinners.' But wisdom is proved right by her deeds" (NIV).

Matthew 26:26-29: "While they were eating, Jesus took *some* bread, and after a blessing, He broke *it* and gave *it* to the disciples, and said, "Take, eat; this is My body." And when He had taken a cup and given thanks, He gave *it* to them, saying, "Drink from it, all of you; for this is My blood of the covenant, which is poured out for many for forgiveness of sins. But I say to you, I will not drink of this fruit of the vine from now on until that day when I drink it new with you in My Father's kingdom'" (NASB).

Mark 14:25: "Truly, I say to you, I will not drink again of the fruit of the vine until that day when I drink it new in the kingdom of God" (NIV).

John 2:7-11: "Jesus told the servants, 'Fill the jars with water.' When the jars had been filled, he said, 'Now dip some out, and take it to the master of ceremonies.' So, the servants followed his instructions. When the master of ceremonies tasted the water that was now wine, not knowing where it had come from (though, of course, the servants knew), he called the bridegroom over. 'A host always serves the best wine first,' he said. 'Then, when everyone has had a lot to drink, he brings out the less expensive wine. But you have kept the best until now!' This miraculous sign at Cana in Galilee was the first time Jesus revealed his glory. And his disciples believed in him".

First Corinthians 6:12: "All things are lawful for me, but not all things are profitable. All things are lawful for me, but I will not be mastered by anything" (NASB).

First Timothy 5:22-23: "Do not be hasty in the laying on of hands, and do not share in the sins of others. Keep yourself pure. Stop drinking only water and use a little wine because of your stomach and your frequent illnesses" (NIV).

Alcohol use as a blessing from God

God blesses us in many ways. His blessings range from physical, material blessings to spiritual blessings and the domains of relationships, career, and finances. Regarding God's blessings within the physical world, Brueggemann notes, "Blessing concerns natural processes that belong to the orbit of creation theology, wherein God's good and fruitful world is celebrated."[28] The Scriptures echo with the truth that wine was one major descriptor of God's blessings as summarized below:

Genesis 27:28: "May God give you of heaven's dew and of earth's richness, an abundance of grain and new wine " (NIV).

Genesis 27:37: "Isaac answered Esau, 'I have made him lord over you and have made all his relatives his servants, and I have sustained him with grain and new wine. So, what can I possibly do for you, my son?'" (NIV).

---

28 Walter Brueggemann, *Reverberations of Faith: A Theological Handbook of Old Testament Themes* (London: Westminster John Knox Press, 2002), 18.

Second Chronicles 2:10: "I will give for your servants, the woodsmen who cut timber, 20,000 cors of crushed wheat, 20,000 cors of barley, 20,000 baths of wine, and 20,000 baths of oil" (NIV).

Isaiah 62:8-9: "The Lord has sworn by his right hand and by his mighty arm: 'Never again will I give your grain as food for your enemies, and never again will foreigners drink the new wine for which you have toiled; but those who harvest it will eat it and praise the Lord, and those who gather the grapes will drink it in the courts of my sanctuary'" (NIV).

Ecclesiastes 9:7: "Go, eat your food with gladness, and drink your wine with a joyful heart, for God has already approved what you do" (NIV).

Jeremiah 31:12: "They will come home and sing songs of joy on the heights of Jerusalem. They will be radiant because of the Lord's good gifts, the abundant crops of grain, new wine, and olive oil, and the healthy flocks and herds. Their life will be like a watered garden, and all their sorrows will be gone".

Joel 2:24: "The threshing floors will again be piled high with grain, and the presses will overflow with new wine and olive oil."

Amos 9:14: "I will bring my exiled people of Israel back from distant lands, and they will rebuild their ruined cities and live in them again. They will plant vineyards and gardens; they will eat their crops and drink their wine ".

Nehemiah 8:10: "Then he said to them, 'Go, eat of the fat, drink of the sweet, and send portions to him who has nothing prepared; for this day is holy to our Lord. Do not be grieved, for the joy of the Lord is your strength'" (NASB).

Alcohol as an offering to God

Alcohol (wine) was also used as a type of offering to God (liquid or drink offering), and was numbered among the other valid offerings, as summarized by the following passages:

Exodus 29:40: "With one of them, offer two quarts of choice flour mixed with one quart of pure oil of pressed olives; also, offer one quart of wine as a liquid offering".

Leviticus 23:13: "…together with its grain offering of two-tenths of an ephah of fine flour mixed with oil—an offering made to the Lord by fire, a pleasing aroma—and its drink offering of a quarter of a hin of wine" (NIV).

Numbers 6:20: "The priest shall then wave them before the Lord as a wave offering; they are holy and belong to the priest, together with the breast that was waved and the thigh that was presented. After that, the Nazirite may drink wine" (NIV).

Numbers 15:5: "With each lamb for the burnt offering or the sacrifice, prepare a quarter of a hin of wine as a drink offering" (NIV).

First Corinthians 10:31: "So whether you eat or drink, or whatever you do, do it all for the glory of God" (NIV).

On the other hand, are dire warnings against the misuse of alcohol.

Alcohol abuse

The definition of what entails alcohol abuse is not based on subjective experience or personal opining, but clear, objective evidence, both biblically and medically. Biblically, the condemnation of alcohol use occurs when the individual loses control of physical and cognitive faculties. This idea of loss of control is taught specifically in Ephesians 5:18: "Don't be drunk with wine, because that will ruin your life. Instead, be filled with the Holy Spirit". The exegetical key to this verse revolves around the use of the phrase "be filled with the Holy Spirit." While this book is not intended to be an in-depth exegesis of what it means to be filled with the Spirit, the Bible presents an undeniable list of the spiritual and character traits of the believer who is filled with the Spirit. In Galatians 5:19-26, we find this list:

> The acts of the flesh are obvious: sexual immorality, impurity and debauchery; idolatry and witchcraft; hatred, discord, jealousy, fits of rage, selfish ambition, dissensions, factions and envy; drunkenness, orgies, and the like. I warn you, as I did before, that those who live like this will not inherit the kingdom of God.

> But the fruit of the Spirit is love, joy, peace, forbearance, kindness, goodness, faithfulness, gentleness and self-control. Against such things there is no law. Those who belong to Christ Jesus have crucified the flesh with its passions and desires. Since we live by the Spirit, let us keep in step with the Spirit. Let us not become conceited, provoking and envying each other (NIV).

In the presence of alcohol abuse and its growing control over the individual's physical, cognitive, and emotional processes, the trajectory of the "acts of the flesh" increases while the "fruit (control) of the Spirit" diminishes. This is a clear observation that has been made by anyone who has experienced a friend or family member "under the influence." Even a cursory study of the controlling and disintegrating effects of alcohol abuse on the human body reveals a portrait of debilitation and hopelessness.[29]

According to Chafer and Walvoord, the Christian is involved in a constant struggle to come under the control of the Holy Spirit, the evidence of which will be the fruit of the Spirit as mentioned above. They assert, however, when this happens, "impressive results" will occur in the Christian life.[30] Boice echoes these sentiments when he notes that the fruit of the Spirit is evidence of the life of Christ and the continuing work of the Holy Spirit to develop the character of Christ within the Christian.[31]

---

29 Jacques Rutzky, *Coyote Speaks: Creative Strategies for Psychotherapists Treating Alcoholics and Addicts* (London: Jason Aronson Inc., 1998), 52-53.

30 Lewis Sperry Chafer and John Walvoord, *Major Bible Themes* (Grand Rapids, MI: Zondervan, 1974), 121-122.

31 James Montgomery Boice, *Foundations of the Christian Faith: A Comprehensive & Readable Theology* (Downers Grove, IL: InterVarsity Press, 1986), 384-385.

The application here is clear; my life will provide evidence as to who or what is controlling my life. If the Holy Spirit, then the fruits of the Spirit; if the flesh, then the fruits of the flesh. This fact is beyond dispute. The following biblical references provide a concise commentary regarding the issue of alcohol abuse:

Alcohol abuse condemned

Isaiah 28:1: "What sorrow awaits the proud city of Samaria—the glorious crown of the drunks of Israel, it sits at the head of a fertile valley, but its glorious beauty will fade like a flower. It is the pride of a people brought down by wine".

Galatians 5:19-21: "Now the deeds of the flesh are evident, which are: immorality, impurity, sensuality, idolatry, sorcery, enmities, strife, jealousy, outbursts of anger, disputes, dissensions, factions, envying, drunkenness, carousing, and things like these, of which I forewarn you, just as I have forewarned you, that those who practice such things will not inherit the kingdom of God" (NASB).

Alcohol abuse as a curse on humanity

Lamentations 4:21-22: "Are you rejoicing in the land of Uz, O people of Edom? But you, too, must drink from the cup of the Lord's anger. You, too, will be stripped naked in your drunkenness. O beautiful Jerusalem, your punishment will end; you will soon return from exile. But Edom, your punishment is just beginning; soon your many sins will be exposed".

Habakkuk 2:15-16: "Woe to you who make your neighbors drink, who mix in your venom even to make *them* drunk so as to look on their nakedness. You will be filled with disgrace rather than honor. Now you yourself drink and expose your *own* nakedness. The cup in the Lord's right hand will come around to you, and utter disgrace will come upon your glory" (NASB).

Alcohol abuse causes cognitive distortions

Proverbs 23:29-33: "Who has anguish? Who has sorrow? Who is always fighting? Who is always complaining? Who has unnecessary bruises? Who has bloodshot eyes? It is the one who spends long hours in the taverns, trying out new drinks. Don't gaze at the wine, seeing how red it is, how it sparkles in the cup, how smoothly it goes down. For in the end it bites like a poisonous snake; it stings like a viper. You will see hallucinations, and you will say crazy things".

Isaiah 28:7: "Now, however, Israel is led by drunks, who reel with wine and stagger with alcohol. The priests and prophets stagger with alcohol and lose themselves in wine. They reel when they see visions and stagger as they render decisions".

Alcohol abuse deteriorates job performance

Proverbs 23:20-21: "Do not carouse with drunkards or feast with gluttons, for they are on their way to poverty, and too much sleep clothes them in rags".

Proverbs 31:4-5: "It is not for kings, O Lemuel, to guzzle wine. Rulers should not crave alcohol. For if they drink, they may forget the law and not give justice to the oppressed".

Alcohol abuse destroys relationships

Proverbs 23:29: "Who has anguish? Who has sorrow? Who is always fighting? Who is always complaining? Who has unnecessary bruises? Who has bloodshot eyes?".

Habakkuk 2:16: "But soon it will be your turn to be disgraced. Come, drink and be exposed. Drink from the cup of the Lord's judgment, and all your glory will be turned to shame".

Alcohol abuse erodes health

Proverbs 23:30-32: "It is the one who spends long hours in the taverns, trying out new drinks. Don't gaze at the wine, seeing how red it is how it sparkles in the cup, how smoothly it goes down. For in the end it bites like a poisonous snake; it stings like a viper. You will see hallucinations, and you will say crazy things".

Hosea 7:5: "On the day of our king, the princes became sick with the heat of wine; He stretched out his hand with scoffers" (NASB).

Alcohol abuse deteriorates morals

Genesis 9:21: "One day he drank some wine he had made, and he became drunk and lay naked inside his tent".

Habakkuk 2:5: "Indeed, wine betrays him; he is arrogant and never at rest. Because he is as greedy as the grave and like death is never satisfied, he gathers to himself all the nations and takes captive all the peoples" (NIV).

Alcohol abuse disqualifies from church leadership

First Timothy 3:2-3: "So a church leader must be a man whose life is above reproach. He must be faithful to his wife. He must exercise self-control, live wisely, and have a good reputation. He must enjoy having guests in his home, and he must be able to teach. He must not be a heavy drinker or be violent. He must be gentle, not quarrelsome, and not love money".

Titus 2:3: "Similarly, teach the older women to live in a way that honors God. They must not slander others or be heavy drinkers. Instead, they should teach others what is good".

Clearly, alcohol use is a two-sided coin. On one side, alcohol use *can* be beneficial and seen as a gift from God, or as an off ring to God. In opposition to this, alcohol misuse *will* destroy one's life;[32] relationships, occupation, finances, health, and spiritual life will all be negatively impacted and slowly erode. West notes, "Christians should learn from the old aphorism about wine: 'A turncoat; first a friend, and then an enemy.'"[33] In many cases, alcohol misuse will bring unwanted, unpleasant, and expensive legal consequences. Inaba and Cohen point out this "two-faced" character of alcohol use:

Because alcohol is one of the oldest and most widespread downers, the world's societies have had the most experience with this

---

32 Darryl S. Inaba and William E. Cohen, *Uppers, Downers, All-Arounders: Physical and Mental Effects of Psychoactive Drugs* (Medford, OR: CNS Publications, 2011), 5.1.

33 Jim West, *Drinking with Calvin and Luther: A History of Alcohol in the Church* (Lincoln, CA: Oakdown, 2003), 26.

drug and have had to adjust to its impacts on health, crime, and domestic violence. The lowering of inhibitions, the loss of physical and emotional control, the strain on the liver, the damage to the fetus of a drinking pregnant woman, all contrast with its beneficial effects of relieving stress, helping the heart in low doses, as a disinfectant, and as a medium for various medicines.[34]

At the core of the fickle face of the effects of alcohol in the life of the believer initially involves "heart development." Shaw observes:

In the heart of an addict, there is a self-centered, sinful, and willful desire to fulfill an appetite that causes him to neglect God-given responsibilities and/or to commit harmful acts toward others and self. Rather than an actual physical heart, the word "heart" in the Bible means the inner essence of mankind that contains all desires, attitudes, emotions, and thinking. The addict's thinking is the initial key that triggers addictive behavior and it must be changed for him to have success battling the addiction.[35]

Church history reveals the fact that there are three positions Christians can have regarding alcohol use: (1) total abstinence, (2) moderation, and (3) "I am not sure" or "I do not care."

Abstinence

Regarding total abstinence, much has been written and asserted, sometimes with an attitude of unyielding fervency. This position regarding alcohol use insists that Christians *must* abstain from all forms of alcoholic beverages.

This is not the same as convictions regarding personal use of alcohol, with no judgment or condemnation on those who disagree. The rigidity and legalistic fervor of this position of abstinence is amazing to behold and study.[36]

---

34 Inaba and Cohen, 4.35-5.46.

35 Mark E. Shaw, *Divine Intervention: Hope and Help for Families of Addicts* (Bemidji: MN: FOCUS Publishing, 2011), vii.

36 Peter Lumpkins, *Alcohol Today: Abstinence in an Age of Indulgence* (Garland, TX: Hannibal Books, 2009), 72-89.

There are a number of reasons for Christian abstinence from the use of alcohol given by proponents of this position. Those reasons are summarized in the following list:

1. The basis of abstention for Christians is that alcoholic drinks have moved from the category of beneficial in the Old Testament times, to the category of grossly harmful and evil in later centuries.

2. The alcoholic content of wine in biblical times was much weaker than the alcoholic content of contemporary alcoholic beverages.[37]

3. The wine industry in biblical times produced much less than the contemporary alcoholic beverage industry.

4. Drunkenness was abhorred in biblical times among most cultures, while today's contemporary culture "winks" at alcohol abuse.[38]

5. The danger of "potential alcoholism." This is one of the warnings issued by proponents of abstinence, that one drink of an alcoholic beverage has the potential to lead down the path of addiction.[39]

6. The Law of Love: abstinence for the sake of others who may stumble because of my use of alcohol. This law is powerfully taught by the apostle Paul in Romans 14:14-19:

I know and am convinced on the authority of the Lord Jesus that no food, in and of itself, is wrong to eat. But if someone believes it is wrong, then for that person it is wrong. And if another believer is distressed by what you eat, you are not acting in love if you eat it. Don't let your eating ruin someone for whom Christ died. Then you will not be criticized for doing something you believe is good. For the Kingdom of God is not a matter of what we eat or drink, but of living a life of goodness and peace and joy in the Holy Spirit. If you serve Christ with this attitude, you will please God, and others will approve of you, too. So then, let us aim for harmony in the church and try to build each other up.

---

37 Randy Jaeggli, *Christians and Alcohol: A Scriptural Case for Abstinence* (Greenville, SC: Bob Jones University Press, 2014), 13-20.

38 Peter Masters, *Should Christians Drink? The Biblical Case for Abstinence* (Swansea, UK: Harcourt Colourprint, 1992), 6-16.

39 Kenneth L. Gentry, Jr., *God Gave Wine: What the Bible Says About Alcohol* (Fountain Inn, SC: Gentry Family Trust, 2015), 131-132.

The issue here is to do nothing to make a "weaker brother" stumble. Whittington pragmatically points out, "If I ignore something that distresses my wife (for example), what does that demonstrate? That I love drinking more than I love her. If that's true, I should stop drinking anyway, because there is a problem, and the problem is not her; it's me."[40]

7. To focus on Bible verses that condemn drunkenness, while minimizing or "explaining away" the verses that seem to focus on the positives of alcohol use (especially the divine blessing of wine or its use as an acceptable offering to God).[41]

A final tendency inherent in much of the strict abstinence position is the application of improper deductive hermeneutical approaches to biblical exegesis, instead of proper inductive hermeneutical principles. Allowing the Scriptures to speak for themselves (inductive: extracting the intended meaning and allowing these facts to form my conclusion), instead of speaking for them (deductive: reading my conclusion, assumptions, or worldview into them) is dangerous hermeneutics.[42] Brauch calls the results of deductive hermeneutics "bifurcation," leading to the error of "selectivity in the use of biblical texts."[43]"[43] He warns, "The danger of this abuse of the Scripture lies in its ignoring or rejecting (either outright or by omission) other parts or passages of Scripture that support a different teaching, or present an alternative perspective, or advocate an opposing view."[44]

Finally, the overarching mood of the abstinence position regarding alcohol use is the almost histrionic emotionalism and spiritual rigidity that seems to penetrate much of the argument.[45]

---

40 Brad Whittington, *What Would Jesus Drink? What the Bible Really Says About Alcohol* (n.c.: Wunderfool Press, 2011), 42.

41 Peter Masters, *Should Christians Drink? The Biblical Case for Abstinence* (Swansea, UK: Harcourt Colourprint, 1992), 16-20.

42 Ibid., 21-27.

43 Manfred T. Brauch, *Abusing Scripture: The Consequences of Misreading the Bible* (Downers Grove, IL: IVP Academic, 2009), 46.

44 Ibid., 47.

45 David Wilkerson, *Sipping Saints: Do Christianity and Drinking Mix?* (Old Tappan, NJ: Spire Books, 1978).

Moderation

The pivotal concern regarding the concept of alcohol use in moderation lies in the challenge to define what exactly is meant by "moderation." Establishing an objectively quantifiable measure as to what represents the boundary between alcohol use and abuse emerges as a critical task. Vallant notes:

> The most compelling empirical evidence against the existence of a sharp distinction between alcohol use and the disorder, alcoholism, has been Cahalan's (1970) study of a national panel of alcohol users, which suggests that drinkers cannot be divided into social drinkers and alcoholics, but that the categories of alcohol users and alcohol abusers merge with each other *depending upon one's definition of abuse.* Alcohol abuse is not black and white; it is gray (italics mine).[46]

Without a clear definition of moderation, this discussion amounts to nothing more than an expression of opinions, which is somewhat akin to one blind lemming citing the opinion of another blind lemming regarding methods of how to avoid walking off a cliff.

The deceptive effects of alcohol abuse can be seen repeatedly in the contemporary culture and church, as well as throughout church history. For example, Luther and Calvin (among many other Reformers), regularly engaged in alcohol use.[47] They stand in church history as undisputed theological giants and primary catalysts for the birth and sustainability of the Protestant Reformation. Their writings head the list of the most monumental theological works in history.[48] However, even a cursory reading of their lives yields the disappointing realization that they may have periodically been guilty of alcohol misuse. That this was reflective of their surrounding socio-historical culture does not minimize their alcohol misuse; they stand

---

46 George E. Vallant, *The Natural History of Alcoholism Revisited* (London: Harvard University Press, 1995), 4.

47 Jim West, *Drinking with Calvin and Luther: A History of Alcohol in the Church* (Lincoln, CA: Oakdown, 2003), 19.

48 Stephen J. Nichols, *Pages from Church History: A Guided Tour of Christian Classics* (Phillipsburg, NJ: P&R Publishing, 2006), 166-171.

squarely in the company of Noah (and others; Genesis 9:7; Matthew 24:38)) in this regard. Luther's tongue-in-cheek definitions of imbibing in too much alcohol are motivation enough to establish a clear, measurable definition of alcohol abuse. He is reported to have provided this murky definition of alcohol abuse when he said, "Drunkenness: when the tongue walks on stilts and reason goes forward under a half sail," and, "If God can forgive me for having crucified Him (Christ) with Masses twenty years running, He can also bear with me for occasionally taking a good drink to honor Him."[49] Luther regularly asserted he drank to "spite the devil."[50] When a copy of Luther's Ninety-Five Theses made their way to Pope Leo X in Rome, the Pope's first reported response was, "All the ramblings of a drunkard German.

___

49 Jim West, *Drinking with Calvin and Luther: A History of Alcohol in the Church* (Lincoln, CA: Oakdown, 2003), 30-31.
50 Ibid., 33.

He will think differently when he
sobers up."[51] The interesting part of
this story is the Pope's first response;
it was not a reference to "more heresy,"
but, rather, a reference to Luther 's
apparent reputation of being a heavy
drinker. This response is especially
enlightening when one reads the
historical records of the heavy drinking
habits of the Papists. The Roman
Catholic Church even created a list of
"beer saints" and "wine saints."[52] Shaff
indirectly references Luther's heavy
alcohol use when he observes, "(Luther
was) swayed by the impulse of the
moment, without regard to logical
consistency or fear of consequences.

His faults as well as his virtues lay on the surface of his German works."[53]

Like Luther, John Calvin also viewed alcohol (wine) as a gift from God
to be enjoyed.[54] He was known to have encouraged receiving wine as a
"salary," and taking wine as payment for others' debts to him. However, he
raged against drunkenness and recognized the difference between alcohol
use and misuse. In his commentary on Psalm 104:15, Calvin warned against
"using drunkenness as a pretext for a new cult based upon abstinence."[55]

Perhaps more than any other Reformer, Calvin understood the
importance of establishing a quantitative definition of the boundary between
alcohol use and misuse. He warned, "If a man knows that he has a weak
head and that he cannot carry three glasses of wine without being overcome,

<hr>

51   Stephen J. Nichols, *Pages from Church History: A Guided Tour of Christian
     Classics* (Phillipsburg, NJ: P&R Publishing, 2006), 150.

52   West, 22.

53   Philip Schaff, *History of the Christian Church,* Vol. 7 (Peabody, MA: Hendrickson
     Publishers, 2011), 732.

54   Jim West, *Drinking with Calvin and Luther: A History of Alcohol in the Church*
     (Lincoln, CA: Oakdown, 2003), 53.

55   Philip Schaff, *History of the Christian Church,* Vol. 7 (Peabody, MA: Hendrickson
     Publishers, 2011), 53.

he then drinks indiscreetly, is he not a hog?'[56] The definition of moderation is transparent regarding function, but opaque in meaning. Again, the need for a quantifiable definition, which I will address later in this book.

"I Am Not Sure, or I Do Not Care."

Sadly, this attitude is evident in the lives of some professing believers, with the result being lives that bear testimonial fruit to the effects of alcohol abuse. This category of belief is one of the primary themes of this book; to encourage the establishment of spiritually healthy beliefs and behaviors in the lives of believers regarding spiritual maturity and its application to decisions regarding alcohol use.

An Arrogant Story

Billy was a middle-aged senior leader within his organization who was facing monumental challenges due to his chronic alcohol abuse. Due to his long history of continuous alcohol abuse, Billy's supervisor directed him to an addiction medicine healthcare provider. His intake assessment yielded a medical diagnosis of Alcohol Use Disorder: Severe, a diagnosis once known as alcoholism. While in the treatment program, Billy gave the impression of being fully engaged. He was participative in all his weekly group therapy sessions, responsive and cooperative in all of his weekly individual therapy sessions, and reportedly attentive and responsive in his psychoeducation class. He also reported attending two to three recovery groups per week in full compliance with his treatment plan requirements. However, one critical deficiency existed regarding Billy's attitude; arrogance and overconfidence permeated his life and perspective. He never got to the point where he admitted he had lost control over his life and that it had become unmanageable. This realization and shift in thinking has to happen before real progress and growth can be made. In fact, this realization summarizes the first step of the Twelve Steps of Alcoholics Anonymous and is foundational to the biblically based Celebrate Recovery program. Because Billy's arrogance was the source of his motivation and determination (i.e., "I

---

56   Ibid., 54.

can do it and I really don't have a problem"), his recovery was undermined. Once his treatment program was complete, along with multiple warnings against arrogance and lack of recognition he had given up control of his life to alcohol abuse, Billy confidently set out on his own, stating, "I hope I never drink too much again." Within days he was back to getting black-out drunk. On one weekend, he became black-out drunk and committed a felony. Waking up in jail the next morning, Billy claimed he did not remember anything from the night before, stating, "I guess I drank too much." Now his life was limited to an eight-foot cell and long-term prison time. All because he was too arrogant to humble himself in the face of the recovery process.

Critical Thought
Humbly accepting and adopting the quantifiable definition of the boundary between alcohol use and abuse is a critical task for the Christian who makes the decision to use alcohol.

Questions for Further Thought

1. *Do you know God's will for your life?*

2. *How sure are you about this?*

3. *What do you do when you are facing an important decision?*

4. *On a scale of 1-10, what level of abundant living are you currently experiencing? What needs to change in your life to increase that number?*

5. *On a scale of 1-10, how satisfi are you with your current level of knowledge of, and obedience to, the Bible? What needs to change in your life to increase that number?*

4

Another View of the Diamond

"Natural Revelation: What Does Science Say About Alcohol Use?"

More Understanding. The overarching testimony of science regarding alcohol use is that *abuse* must be avoided due to the destructive effects of alcohol if abused frequently and heavily enough. Alcohol abuse, over time, will negatively and destructively impact all areas of life. This comprehensive and progressive eroding of all areas of life is predictable, quantifiable, and documented in both natural and special revelation. Amazingly, while alcohol has been embraced by Western culture as its drug of choice, the effects of alcohol abuse and accompanying withdrawal are the most damaging and dangerous *of any other drug*, oftentimes fatal.[1]

The following list provides a summary discussion of these areas of life impacted by alcohol abuse:

Physiology

Human physiology is comprehensively impacted by alcohol abuse. Over time, the destruction of the physiology of the human body is total. According to Coombs and Howatt:

Alcohol effects virtually every organ system in the body. Both acute and chronic intoxication have unique consequences on physiology and quality of life. Alcohol increases the risk for injuries through the impairment of cognitive and psychomotor functioning. It decreases reaction time and impairs sensory processing, motor

---

1   H. Thomas Milhorn, Jr., *Drug and Alcohol Abuse: The Authoritative Guide for Parents, Teachers, and Counselors* (New York: Plenum Press, 1994), 251, 254.

control, attention…increases the risk for injury or death from fire and suicide. It causes social and legal problems, interacts with medications, and creates birth defects as well as the longterm health problems (including)…liver disease, cardiovascular disease, and cancer.[2]

Clearly, alcohol abuse produces toxic effects on the entire body. This fact is beyond dispute.

Specific damage and destruction to the body include liver disease, cardiovascular disease, cancer, and neurological deterioration.[3]

One of my recent patients was an upper management senior leader who was medically evacuated from an overseas assignment due to having developed an alcohol addiction. After his intake assessment, he was enrolled in a treatment program designed to treat alcohol dependency. While he was a resounding treatment success over the next 120 days, he slowly developed related health problems that revolved around a failing liver due to his chronic alcohol abuse. He was hospitalized and treated for his failing medical condition. Having spent nearly twenty-five years working hard and sacrificing for his career and (in his mind) family, his only desire was to recover so he could spend all of his time with his wife and children. He reported feeling guilt and shame because he was forced to spend so much time away from his family due to career obligations that involved consistent travel and extensive time away from his family. His overarching desire at this point in his life was to "make up for all that time away from my family," looking forward especially to being there to watch and participate in the lives of his children as they developed and grew up. He stated to me one day, "I didn't think my drinking was so bad at the time because others around me drank more than me. But now, looking back on my life and career, especially recently, now that I understand the addiction process and negative effects my heavy drinking has had on my body, I see why I am having these physical problems now. My biggest fear is dying and not being there to see my children grow up."

---

2   Robert Holman Coombs and William A. Howatt, *The Addiction Counselor's Desk Reference* (Hoboken, N.J.: John Wiley and Sons, 2005), 5.

3   Ibid., 4.

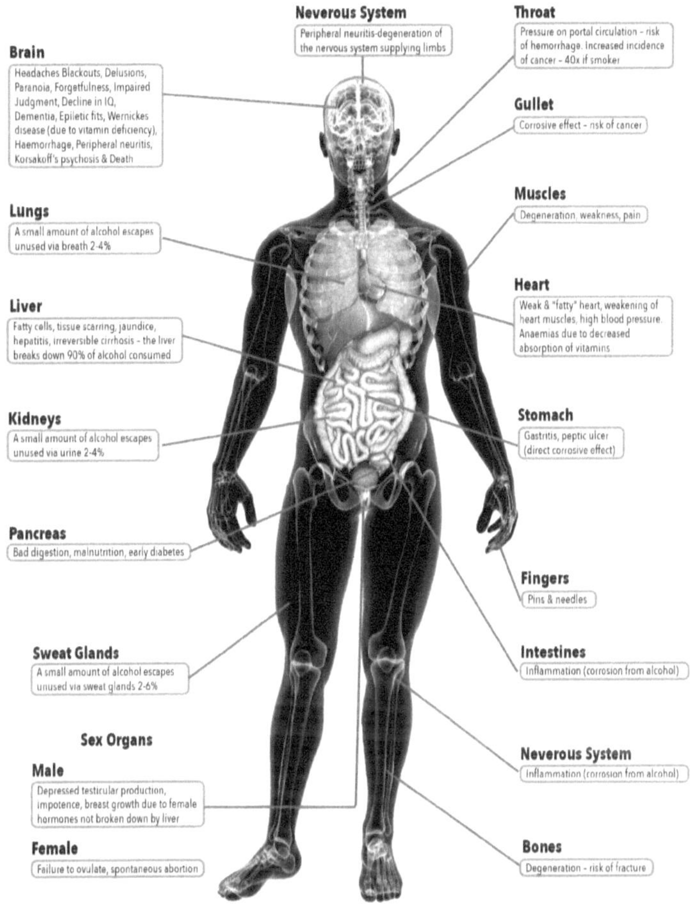

This observation from him (and so many others) reveals the deceptive nature of alcohol abuse. Without a quantifiable boundary established between alcohol use and abuse, things don't seem too bad *at the time*, but hindsight is always 20/20. We see *now* with the understanding we wished we would have had in the past.

Neurology

The human brain is often overlooked in terms of its critical importance in providing full spectrum management of bodily functions, both voluntary and involuntary. The human brain may be accurately described as residing within a chemical soup that is perfectly balanced for optimal functioning, and highly vulnerable to the destructive influence and impact of alcohol abuse when introduced into the neurological environment. Alterations in behavior and decision-making judgment, irreversible destruction of brain cells, "sludging" (a decrease in brain protein synthesis), brain shrinkage, peripheral neuropathy, illogic, psychosis, disorientation, memory erosion, and related disease catalysis are only some of the derogatory effects alcohol abuse has on the human brain. From a spiritual and moral perspective, alcohol abuse creates lying, deception, secret-keeping, isolation, and dysfunctional thinking that imposes a frame of unreality.[4] In his classic work in brain health, Dr. Daniel Amen provides this warning:

> You don't have to be a heavy drinker to hurt your brain. Even moderate amounts of alcohol can affect brain function. Studies show that people who drink every day have smaller brains than nondrinkers. When it comes to the brain, size matters. Excessive drinking lowers activity in the PFC (Prefrontal Cortex), the area responsible for judgment, forethought, and planning. That's why people make such stupid decisions when they have had a few too many, like stopping at the burger joint at three o'clock in the morning when they're trying to lose weight, having unprotected sex with someone they just met at a bar, or driving when they've had too much to drink.[5]

I like to point out to many of my patients that alcohol makes liars and deceivers of us all. It whispers in the ear of the drinker, "Hey, it's okay to drive home. You're good. Your drinking tonight has not hurt you." Most of my patients who are in treatment due to alcohol-related driving incidents say the same thing: "I thought I was good, but I guess I wasn't."

Focusing on brain health provides the key to clear thinking and low-risk decision-making regarding alcohol use.

---

4   James E. Royce and David Scratchley, *Alcoholism and Other Drug Problems* (New York: The Free Press, 1996), 71.

5   Daniel G. Amen, *Change Your Brain, Change Your Body* (New York: Harmony Books, 2010), 24.

Relationships

The destruction of relationships: friendships, marriages, and families, resulting from alcohol abuse is indisputable. Marital conflict, domestic violence, divorce, and child abuse (physical, emotional, verbal, and sexual) are characteristic and often co-occurring with alcohol abuse. For children of alcoholics, the development of dysfunctional emotional, relational, and thought processes and patterns is foreseeable, unsurprising, and well-documented.[6] These dysfunctional emotional and thought processes that negatively impact relationships has been labeled "codependency," a maladaptive and problematic way of seeing identity and self-worth outside of the self.[7]

A recurring reason given by some of my patients in answer to the question, "Why have you come to see me today?" is "My spouse demanded I get some help for my drinking." While this is, generally, a good thing that leads to a time of effective treatment (hopefully), most spouses have no idea how they can support their significant other who is personally experiencing the disconcerting challenges attached to the removal of alcohol from their life. Some spouses, either consciously or subconsciously, seek to function as a "sobriety policeman or warden." Others see themselves as an "alcohol-use detective." Yet others may respond as a "rescuer," seeking to minimize their spouse's behavior out of compassion or misplaced loyalty.

Regardless of relational dynamics, one thing is abundantly clear; alcohol abuse and drunkenness is not limited in its destructive effects. Not only is the individual affected, but everybody surrounding the alcoholic is negatively affected.

Career

Elevated alcohol abuse over time has been the destructive power behind the loss of jobs and careers. The corrosive impact of chronic alcohol abuse on the individual's ability to think or physically function normally,

---

6   H. Thomas Milhorn, Jr., *Drug and Alcohol Abuse: The Authoritative Guide for Parents, Teachers, and Counselors* (New York: Plenum Press, 1994), 221-223.

7   Tim Clinton and Eric Scalise, *Addictions and Recovery Counseling* (Grand Rapids, MI: Baker Books, 2013), 72-73.

in combination with the resultant deterioration of healthy sleep patterns, serves to increase lateness or illness-related absence from work, decreasing productivity, elevated anxiety due to probable withdrawal symptoms or cravings, and deteriorating work relationships, are all work-environment-related signs of alcohol abuse.

According to the DSM-5:

> Craving for alcohol is indicated by a strong desire to drink that makes it difficult to think of anything else and that often results in the onset of drinking. School and job performance may also suffer either from the aftereffects of drinking or from actual intoxication at school or on the job; childcare or household responsibilities may be neglected; and alcohol-related absences may occur from school or work. The individual may use alcohol in physically hazardous circumstances (e.g. driving an automobile, swimming, or operating machinery while intoxicated).[8]

Some of my patients are military members who are being discharged from the service under "less than honorable conditions," due to their high-risk alcohol use that has led to violations of both civilian and military law. Some of these patients have more than twenty years of service, and are experiencing the loss of a career of lifetime accomplishments, retirement benefits, and private and public humiliation.

Finances

Financial catastrophe is another result of alcohol abuse. The obvious connection between job or career loss and resultant loss of income begins the domino effect of destitution leading to poverty; the financial strain triggered by the individual's need to purchase increasing levels of alcohol adds to the drain of personal resources; driving under the influence of alcohol will produce unwanted, humiliating, and very expensive legal costs; and associated medical costs in treating the debilitating physical and mental damage done by alcohol abuse can be astronomical.

---

8 *Diagnostic and Statistical Manual of Mental Disorders,* 5th ed. (Arlington, VA: American Psychiatric Association, 2013), 492, 496.

Focusing solely on the cost of purchasing alcohol, the financial cost is staggering. It is estimated in America alone alcohol use is a $50 billion annual industry. This amounts to more than all non-alcoholic beverages *combined*.[9]

Spiritual Growth

Alcohol abuse will negate any possibility of spiritual growth. The foundational issue is *control*. Over time, alcohol abuse progressively takes over control of the body and brain, slowly neutralizing spiritual influence in the life of the Christian. This is the issue the apostle Paul addresses in Ephesians 5:18 when he exhorts, "Don't be drunk with wine, because that will ruin your life. Instead, be filled with the Holy Spirit". The control of alcohol abuse over our life is, perhaps, best illustrated in Proverbs 23:29-35:

[29] Who has anguish? Who has sorrow?
  Who is always fighting? Who is always complaining?
  Who has unnecessary bruises? Who has bloodshot eyes?
[30] It is the one who spends long hours in the taverns,
  trying out new drinks.
[31] Don't gaze at the wine, seeing how red it is,
  how it sparkles in the cup, how smoothly it goes down.
[32] For in the end it bites like a poisonous snake;
  it stings like a viper.
[33] You will see hallucinations,
  and you will say crazy things.
[34] You will stagger like a sailor tossed at sea,
  clinging to a swaying mast.
[35] And you will say, "They hit me, but I didn't feel it.
  I didn't even know it when they beat me up.
  When will I wake up
  so I can look for another drink?"

One of the recurring patterns of alcohol abuse is *consequences*. The ability to engage in "consequential thinking" is a hallmark of sober, spiritually

---

9   *Quora,* accessed April 24, 2019. https://www.quora.com/
How-much-do-Americans-spend-on-booze-each-year.

grounded thinking. The realization that doing one thing will lead to another (an unintended effect), represents a "domino-effect," perfectly illustrated in instances of alcohol abuse. Royce and Scratchley note:

> In addition to its short-term effects on driving and other behaviors, alcohol is a prime cause10 of chronic damage to nearly every organ in the body, for six months to three years, and often irreversibly. Death in alcoholics is due to the following causes in order of frequency: cardiovascular issues (heart attacks and strokes), cancer, suicide, accidents, cirrhosis of the liver.[10]

Some may argue that these are physical, not spiritual effects. However, if the apostle Paul was correct when he called the human body "the temple of the Holy Spirit" (First Corinthians 6:15-20), then intentionally harming my body can certainly be classified as sin and a destroyer of spiritual health. The idea of my actions having a "domino-effect" in my life cannot be overstated; all of my actions have consequences. This includes my decisions regarding alcohol use.

Alcohol abuse that leads to drunkenness commonly leads to deteriorating health and death, violence, law-breaking, high-risk sexual activity and adultery, marital conflict or dissolution, child abuse, and the loss of friendships, personal possessions, career, finances, and spiritual closeness with God. This cause-effect relationship between alcohol abuse and its related consequences is a familiar story, experienced and told by many in recovery groups such as Alcoholics Anonymous and Celebrate Recovery.

A Spiritual Story

Henry was a senior manager, having spent decades sacrificially building his career. Based on his proven successes and powerful position, Henry was viewed as a resounding success. However, he had an alcohol-use problem that had been increasing over the years. Up to this point he was able to hide it, primarily because he worked in a high alcohol-use culture. If one thing is true

---

10   James E. Royce and David Scratchley, *Alcoholism and Other Drug Problems* (New York: Free Press, 1996), 62-76.

of his work culture, it is that alcohol flows freely and heavily. But his alcohol-abuse had caught up to Henry. Driving home from a holiday social event where Henry had drunk his usual eight to ten drinks, he was stopped by local law enforcement for erratic driving. He was breathalyzed with the resultant blood-alcohol content of 0.24, more than three times the legal limit. Henry was arrested and charged with DUI. The CEO (Henry's boss), referred Henry to a substance abuse treatment, and Henry began the program. During the ensuing months of group and individual therapy, Henry recounted growing up in an active Christian family, attending church weekly, being involved in his church youth group, and regularly engaging in personal Bible study and prayer times. He admitted, "It has been quite a number of years since I paid that much attention to my spiritual life," and thought, perhaps, this had something to do with his current dilemma. Near the end of his ninety-day treatment program, Henry came to the conclusion that he needed to make a dramatic shift in how he was living his life. He made the decision to re-embrace his spiritual heritage, and to begin once again doing the things he used to do when his life was happy, successful, and drama-free. Henry confessed to his therapist on his treatment discharge day that he intended to turn over ownership of his heart and life to God and the control of the Holy Spirit, and to once again dig into the Word of God through personal and corporate Bible studies. One year later, Henry was still firm in his recommitment to spirituality and his relationship with Christ and His Word, and reported continual recovery success.

Critical Thought

Seeking the way of wisdom as revealed in the Bible, and control of the Holy Spirit, must be a central life-focus for Christian decision-making.

Questions for Further Thought

On a scale of 1-10, how satisfied are you in these areas of your life? What is one change that you could make to improve this number?

1. *Physiology (your physical condition):*

2. *Neurology (your thinking processes and abilities):*

3. *Relationships (marriage, family, work, and friends/ neighbors):*

4. *Career:*

5. *Finances:*

6. *Spiritual Growth (time, effort, and fruit you see in your life):*

5

───᠁───

Taking Action

"Integrate the Bible and Science into Your Life"

Integration. The debate between the church and science has a long and storied history of mutual mistrust and separation. However, the concept of the unity of truth clearly demonstrates this position is unnecessary. The Bible unambiguously teaches that God is revealed in creation, while science consistently supports many biblical teachings regarding creation. Christians must, therefore, intentionally integrate all of God's truth into our lives. There is nothing to fear from scientific observations, only, in some cases, the interpretation drawn from those observations. The Bible remains the final filter through which all truth must be measured and verified.

When Christians apply this principle of *intentional integration* of all truth into their lives, then decisions regarding alcohol use will be balanced in a way that avoids sin and the surrender of control of body, mind, and spirit to something other than the control of the Holy Spirit.

The Bible uses the imperative mood to present commands regarding Christian behavior, including both acts of commission and omission. Commands to do or avoid something (including decisions regarding alcohol use) proliferate throughout the pages of Scripture. According to Boyce, (regarding commands and prohibitions), by far the largest number (1,357 or 83 percent) belong to this category, which includes both positive and negative commands. The latter, often listed separately under the term "prohibitions," are introduced by some form of the negative particle "μή" (may). There are 188 of them; here they are simply included under the term "commands." Commands include a broad spectrum of concepts: injunctions, orders, admonitions, exhortations, ranging from authoritarian dictates (e.g., a centurion ordering his soldier to go or come, Matthew 8:9), to the act of teaching (Jesus' Sermon on the Mount, Matthew 5:2, cf. 12ff). Commands are distinguished from requests as "telling" is from "asking."[1]

In his "Be" series of Bible study books, Wiersbe frames the biblical use of the imperative in very practical terms, applying the various biblical commands and prohibitions to the Christian life, encouraging commitment to Christ, obedience to the Bible, spiritual strength, and perseverance in the Christian life. In his work *Be Committed*, he presents a study of the lives of two biblical heroines, Ruth and Esther, and observes, "(I am commanded) to be faithful in my service to the glory of the Lord. At an hour in history when it's easy to compromise and even to quit, these two heroines of the faith tell me to be committed to the Lord and to do the will of God, come what may."[2]

The absolute requirement for believers to obey God and His Word is a tapestry that weaves its way throughout the pages of the Bible as follows:

- God reminds the nation of Israel to obey Him and realize the blessings of being God's "treasured possession" (Exodus 19:5).
- In Deuteronomy 11:1, we are reminded to keep God's commands "always."
- In John 15:9, Jesus reminds us to "remain in my love," contextually a direct reference to the dynamics of His love for us, a love characterized by sacrifice, submission, and commitment to His mission of atonement.
- One of the most powerful verses that can be applied to combating the cognitive challenges involved in alcohol abuse is Second Corinthians 10:5: "We destroy arguments and every lofty opinion raised against the knowledge of God, and take every thought captive to obey Christ" (ESV).
- In Revelation 14:12, Christians are reminded of the absolute necessity of "obeying his commands and maintaining their faith in Jesus". The somber reminder here is that the quality of my obedience to God is a direct reflection of the seriousness of my faith in Christ.

---

1   James L. Boyce, "A Classification of Imperatives: A Statistical Study," *Grace Theological Journal*, 8, (1987): 36.

2   Warren W. Wiersbe, *Be Committed* (Wheaton, IL: Victor Books, 1993), 7.

Clearly, the need for integrating *all* truth into my life functions as a protective factor in my life, especially regarding decisions I make regarding alcohol use. Medical science has established a definition of, and quantifiable boundary between, alcohol use and abuse, low risk versus high-risk use of alcohol. And the Bible has described God's attitude toward alcohol abuse; it is an egregious sin and robs the believer of spiritual intimacy with God due to its degrading and deteriorating effects.

A Leadership Story

Joshua enjoyed a leadership position managing nearly 250 employees. As a graduate of a prestigious school, he was extremely popular among both his former classmates and current co-workers. Because of his integrity and leadership, he was beloved and trusted by all.

While attending a spiritual growth seminar focused on decisions regarding alcohol use, Joshua was exposed to both biblical and secular truths of which he was previously unaware. He was a regular attender at the local executives' Christian fellowship, church worship services, and Bible studies, and professed to being a committed Christian, willing to share his faith when given the opportunity. However, he never took the time to participate in an in-depth study of what general and special revelation have to say about alcohol abuse. This was his first seminar that dealt with this topic. During the training, Joshua was fully attentive and engaged. At the end of the training, and during the feedback and discussion phase, Joshua shared the following statement with a great deal of awe and amazement: "I always knew the Bible talked a little bit about alcohol, but I had no idea it had such in-depth teaching about this...and the connection to spiritual maturity and medical facts is especially interesting. I intend to study this further and want to share it with my friends who drink, especially a couple of other executives who are having problems with alcohol abuse."

Critical Thought

*Knowing and applying integrated truth
to the Christian life is crucial for making
wise decisions regarding alcohol use*

Questions for Further Thought

1. *How satisfied are you with your current level of biblical knowledge regarding alcohol use? What needs to change?*

2. *How satisfied are you with your current level of medical knowledge regarding alcohol use? What needs to change?*

3. *How open are you to integrating medical knowledge about alcohol use into your spiritual life?*

4. *When you think of "secular truth," what do you feel?*

5. *When you hear "secular truth" cited, what level of authority do you give to it?*

6

Commitment: Having a Clear Goal

"Make a Wise Decision Based on Knowledge and Conviction"

Commitment. According to the *Merriam-Webster Dictionary* (2018), the meaning of commitment is "the state or an instance of being obligated or emotionally impelled." Powerful synonyms include "attachment, dedication, and loyalty." For the Christian, commitment to God's revealed Word and plan for life includes the related ideas of being attached to God, dedicated to spiritual growth and the spiritual maturity process, and loyalty to God and His purpose in our lives, all of which emerges out of a deep obligation and emotional dynamics that impel us to reach the goal of attaining "the measure of the stature of the fullness of Christ" (Ephesians 4:13).

Biblically, this meaning is best illustrated in the words of Christ. Jesus lays a serious challenge at the feet of His disciples in Luke 9:22-26 with these words:

And he said, "The Son of Man must suffer many things and be rejected by the elders, the chief priests and the teachers of the law, and he must be killed and on the third day be raised to life." Then he said to them all: "Whoever wants to be my disciple must deny themselves and take up their cross daily and follow me. For whoever wants to save their life will lose it, but whoever loses their life for me will save it. What good is it for someone to gain the whole world, and yet lose or forfeit their very self? Whoever is ashamed of me and my words, the Son of Man will be ashamed of them when he comes in his glory and in the glory of the Father and of the holy angels" (NIV).

Jesus concisely and clearly identifies the three key expectations and tasks for every person claiming to follow Him (Luke 9:23): (1) denial of self, (2) take up the cross daily, and (3) follow Him. This spiritual equation eliminates the possibility of the modern concept of being a "nominal" Christian. The divine reality is that all believers are required to give full expression of commitment to Christ *every day*. This is really intended to be a moment-by-moment application of faith and obedience that transcends every area of life and all requisite decisions. This includes decisions made regarding alcohol use.

According to Morris:

The follower of Jesus must *deny himself* (not just his sins, himself; he cannot be self-centered). There is nothing self-indulgent about being a Christian. The disciples had probably seen a man *take up his cross*, and they knew what it meant. When a man from one of their villages took up a cross and went off with a little band of Roman soldiers, he was on a one-way journey. He would not be back. Taking up the cross meant the utmost in self-denial. This is Luke's first use of the word *cross* and it comes with striking effect. Christ's follower has died to a whole way of life (cf. 14:27). Luke tells us that this is not something that can be finished and got out of the way: it must be done *daily* (cf. First Corinthians 15:31). So, says Jesus, will he *follow me*.[1]

The word for "deny" in v. 23 is ἀρνέομαι (arneomai), and includes additional shades of meaning to "repudiate or disown," further illuminating the portrait of faith expected in the Christian life. Furthermore, the verbal form of this word (ἀρνησάσθω, arnasastho), is in the imperative voice, signifying a command from Christ, indicating Christians *must* apply this level of commitment in all life's circumstances and related decisions.[2] Kittel provides this piercing commentary on this idea of personal denial being foundational to Christian commitment: "I must not confess myself

---

1   Leon Morris, *Luke: An Introduction and Commentary,* Vol. 3 (Downers Grove, IL: InterVarsity Press, 1988), 188-189.

2   A. L. Lukaszewski and M. Dubis, M. *The Lexham Syntactic Greek New Testament: Expansions and Annotations* (Logos Bible Software reference, 2009), Luke 9:23.

and my own being, nor cling to myself, but abandon myself in a radical renunciation of myself, and not merely of my sins. I must no longer seek to establish my life of myself but resolutely accept death and allow myself to be established by Christ in discipleship."[3]

Additionally, the cross was a familiar figure in Palestine. It was rising before Jesus as His destiny. Each man has his own cross to meet and bear.[4] The cross was a clear reference to the execution and death of a convicted criminal in the Roman system of justice. When Jesus tells us we must "take up the cross," He is telling us we must execute the self and its self-centered desires, and follow the way leading to death, death to self and a life of devotion to Christ.

A second familiar and primary New Testament passage presents a sober description of the spiritual commitment expected of every Christian. In Luke 14:26, Jesus' definition of the commitment required of His disciples emerges out of these incisive words: "If anyone comes to me and does not hate his own father and mother and wife and children and brothers and sisters and even his own life, he is not able to be my disciple." Commenting on this passage and concept of radical biblical commitment, Gough states:

Being aware of the extreme demands, which following him would place upon his disciples, and knowing that only total commitment in a life of full and complete submission to his will would enable his disciples to persevere faithfully, Jesus called for undivided allegiance on their part. This meant that all other allegiances and affections must be subordinated to the allegiance and devotion that the disciples would give their one supreme Master and Lord. His will would dominate their wills, even to the extent that should the solicitations of the dearest and closest relative come into conflict with loyalty to his Master, the disciple must take the latter course at the cost of separation from the loved one if need be. He might

---

3   G. Kittel, G. W. Bromiley, and G. Friedrich, eds., *Theological Dictionary of the New Testament*, Vol. 1 (Grand Rapids, MI: Eerdmans, electronic ed.), 471.

4   A. T. Robertson, *Word Pictures in the New Testament* (Nashville, TN: Broadman Press., 1933), note on Luke 9:23.

be called upon to give up his very life in the pursuance of the Master's will for him.[5]

In a country like contemporary America, where Christians are constantly bombarded with distractions, unhealthy choices, and a virtual absence of persecution or martyrdom, daily challenges to the essence of being a follower of Christ persist and transcend all other considerations in life. This current state of spiritual affairs removes the urgency from living a moment-by-moment absolute attachment and loyalty to God amid the expectations of discipleship. Jesus' first-century disciples would be continually challenged for their faith, often giving up their very lives as martyrs for the sake of Christ.[6] Today in America, we are not currently challenged like this. However, based on the visible currents of evolving world events and the proliferation of a growing anti-Christian mentality, the challenges of first-century Christians will soon be the experience of the twenty-first century church. Manser gives this simple, practical definition, "Commitment to God arises from faith in his promises, is expressed in worship and adoration, and *leads to obedience to his commands*" (italics mine).[7]

In his classic work *Basic Christianity*, John Stott insightfully presents the Christian life as a series of commitments, beginning with knowing Christ as Savior and continuing into the subsequent life of the individual believer, intended to be lived in obedience to God's Word and will. This demands absolute commitment. Jesus used the word "daily" to identify the intended intensity of this commitment. In this regard, Stott proclaims:

In order to follow Christ, we have to deny ourselves, to crucify ourselves, to lose ourselves. The full inexorable demand of Jesus Christ is now laid bare. He does not call us to a sloppy self-centeredness, but to a vigorous, absolute commitment. He calls us to lives under his control. This includes our career. God has

---

5   L. F. Gough, "A Study of Luke 14:26: Jesus Calls His Disciples to a Life of Supreme Commitment," *Ashland Theological Journal, Volume* 3, (1970), 228.

6   John Foxe, *Foxe's Book of Martyrs* (London: John Day, 1563).

7   M. H. Manser, *Dictionary of Bible Themes: The Accessible and Comprehensive Tool for Topical Studies.* (London: Martin Manser, 2009).

a purpose for every life. Our business is to discover it and do it. God's plan may be different from our parents' or our own. If he is wise, the Christian will do nothing rash or reckless.[8]

Aside from the biblical commands condemning alcohol abuse and drunkenness (see Appendix 1), the idea of who or what is controlling my life is a principal theme, establishing boundaries for comprehensive commitment to Christ and living the abundant Christian life. A fundamental passage that illustrates these principles is Romans 6:17-18: "But thanks be to God that, though you used to be slaves to sin, you have come to obey from your heart the pattern of teaching that has now claimed your allegiance. You have been set free from sin and have become slaves to righteousness" (NIV).

A related concept that can be argued is another synonym of commitment: *spirituality*. This idea has received increasing interest in the contemporary world, with wide ranging meaning. For the Christian, *commitment* and *spirituality* are overlapping ideas, both related to living a life of resolute physical, emotional, and spiritual loyalty to God and obedience to His revealed Word. In this regard, McGrath and Packer explain:

> But what is spirituality? How is this word to be understood? It draws on the Hebrew word *ruach*, a rich term that is usually translated as "spirit," but which includes a range of meanings, intending beyond this to include such ideas as "breath" and "wind." To talk about "the spirit" is to discuss what gives life and animation to someone. Spirituality is thus about the life of faith, what drives and motivates it, and what people find helpful in sustaining and developing it. It is about that which animates the life of believers, and urges them on to deepen and perfect that which at present has only begun.[9]

Regardless of what word or synonym one chooses to describe the mutual ideas of commitment and spirituality, the theological principle of

---

8   John Stott, *Basic Christianity* (Downers Grove, IL: IVP Books, 1971), 142.

9   Alister E. McGrath and James I. Packer, eds., *Zondervan Handbook of Christian Beliefs* (Grand Rapids, MI: The Zondervan Corporation, 2005), 289.

sanctification incorporates all of these concepts into an idea of progressive holiness. This is a spiritual growth process that ultimately leads to spiritual maturity with an accompanying perspective we may apply to decisions regarding alcohol use. Ryrie provides the following insight:

> The second aspect of sanctification concerns the present experiential or progressive work of continuing to be set apart during the whole of our Christian lives. Every command and exhortation to holy living concerns progressive sanctification (First Peter 1:16)…In the process of progressive sanctification, several agents are involved. It was to the Father that our Lord prayed that He would sanctify us through the truth (John 17:17; First Thessalonians 5:23). Thus the Bible becomes an indispensable foundation for our sanctification. How else could we know for sure what pleases a holy God except through His Word? … It is by the Spirit that we put to death the deeds of the body (Romans 8:13) … ignites love in our hearts (Romans 5:5), changes us from glory to glory to make us more like Christ (Second Corinthians 3:18) … and produces in us Christlikeness, which is the goal of sanctification (Galatians 5:22-23).[10]

Knowledge of, and commitment to, the extensive truth God has revealed regarding the victorious Christian life and conviction of one's personal stance regarding alcohol use, are essential tasks for every Christian. The following specific questions and considerations must be contemplated in order to reach a biblically balanced, healthy conclusion regarding alcohol use.

1. What does my conscience say?
2. What does the Bible teach?
3. What does medicine and science teach?
4. What does my current health demand?
5. What does my family history reveal?
6. What do my immediate family members think about this?

---

10 Charles C. Ryrie, *Basic Theology: A Popular Systematic Guide to Understanding Biblical Truths* (Chicago: Moody Press, 1999), 442-443.

7. Will my alcohol use cause another believer to stumble?
8. Am I serving in a position of spiritual leadership?
9. Do I understand the quantifiable boundary between use and abuse?
10. Will alcohol use negatively impact any part of my life?

Based on these questions, below is a suggested decision-making matrix to assist in this process:

Decision-Making Matrix for Alcohol Use

Question	Yes	No
1. Will use violate my conscience?		
2. Do I believe the Bible condemns use?		
3. Does medicine and science condemn use?		
4. Do I have a medical condition that could be harmed by use?		
5. Do I have a family history of abuse or dependence?		
6. Are any of my immediate family members opposed to use?		
7. Do I risk causing another believer to stumble or be offended by my use?		
8. Am I serving in a position of spiritual leadership?		
9. Am I confused as to when use becomes abuse?		
10. Will use create risk for me in any of the following areas of my life: work, legal, social, financial, health, or spiritual?		
*Conclusion: If I answered "yes" to any of these questions, I should prayerfully reflect on the possibility of living an alcohol-free life without judging or imposing my conviction on others who may believe differently.		

Author: Dr. Guy E. Glad, 2019

> ### Critical Thought
> *Commitment involves intentionally seeking God's will and His best for my life in all of my decisions, including decisions regarding alcohol use*

Questions for Further Thought

1. *How much thought have you given regarding alcohol use?*

2. *What is the authority you use to make decisions in your life?*

3. *How important is it for you to know and follow biblically based spiritual principles?*

4. *How much knowledge do you have of medical principles surrounding alcohol use?*

5. *What medical conditions do you have that impact your decisions regarding alcohol use?*

7

If It Isn't My Way...

"Accept Others Who May Not Have the Same Convictions"

Acceptance. Taking a non-judgmental attitude toward others who do not share your convictions is a function of spiritual maturity and vehicle of God's grace. Accepting the fact that there exists more than one attitude toward, and allowance for, alcohol use for Christians, is a critical task reflecting spiritual maturity and understanding of God's grace, His revealed will, and the integration of special and natural revelation regarding dynamics of alcohol use.

The relationship between the abstinence and moderation camps must be characterized by peace, patience, understanding, and grace. Freedom in Christ is the final principle that must rule the day. Both positions, however, agree with the biblically based teaching that alcohol abuse amounts to malignant sin and progressive decay. The Bible is transparently clear on its prohibition against Christians judging one another; doctrinal purity is one thing, freedom in Christ is another. The following verses (NIV) summarize this prohibition against judging others:

Matthew 7:1-5: Do not judge, or you too will be judged. For in the same way you judge others, you will be judged, and with the measure you use, it will be measured to you. "Why do you look at the speck of sawdust in your brother's eye and pay no attention to the plank in your own eye? How can you say to your brother, 'Let me take the speck out of your eye,' when all the time there is a plank in your own eye? You hypocrite, first take the plank out of your own eye, and then you will see clearly to remove the speck from your brother's eye."

Luke 6:37-42: Do not judge, and you will not be judged. Do not condemn, and you will not be condemned. Forgive, and you will be forgiven. Give, and it will be given to you. A good measure, pressed down, shaken together and running over, will be poured into your lap. For with the measure you use, it will be measured to you. He also told them this parable: "Can the blind lead the blind? Will they not both fall into a pit? The student is not above the teacher, but everyone who is fully trained will be like their teacher. Why do you look at the speck of sawdust in your brother's eye and pay no attention to the plank in your own eye? How can you say to your brother, 'Brother, let me take the speck out of your eye,' when you yourself fail to see the plank in your own eye? You hypocrite, first take the plank out of your eye, and then you will see clearly to remove the speck from your brother's eye."

James 4:11-12: Brothers and sisters, do not slander one another. Anyone who speaks against a brother or sister or judges them speaks against the law and judges it. When you judge the law, you are not keeping it, but sitting in judgment on it. There is only one Lawgiver and Judge, the one who is able to save and destroy. But you—who are you to judge your neighbor?

Dockery reminds us:

Harmonious relationships are important. Believers should live without judging others and without influencing others to violate their consciences. Not only should the mature not hinder the weak with their freedom, but the weak must avoid restricting those who have discovered Christian freedom. Mutual love and respect are the marks of true disciples of Christ.[1]

One inevitable result of judging others is the creation of division in the church as the spiritual body of Christ. Division is another biblical prohibition that must be avoided at all costs and eliminated from the

---

1   D. S. Dockery, "The Pauline Letters." In D. S. Dockery, ed., *Holman Concise Bible Commentary* (Nashville, TN: Broadman & Holman Publishers, 1998), 550.

Christian life. Again, this prohibition is clearly demonstrated throughout the pages of Scripture (NIV):

Romans 16:17-19: I urge you, brothers and sisters, to watch out for those who cause divisions and put obstacles in your way that are contrary to the teaching you have learned. Keep away from them. For such people are not serving our Lord Christ, but their own appetites. By smooth talk and flattery they deceive the minds of naive people. Everyone has heard about your obedience, so I rejoice because of you; but I want you to be wise about what is good, and innocent about what is evil.

First Corinthians 1:10, 12: I appeal to you, brothers and sisters, in the name of our Lord Jesus Christ, that all of you agree with one another in what you say and that there be no divisions among you, but that you be perfectly united in mind and thought. My brothers and sisters, some from Chloe's household have informed me that there are quarrels among you. What I mean is this: One of you says, "I follow Paul"; another, "I follow Apollos"; another, "I follow Cephas"; still another, "I follow Christ."

First Corinthians 11:18-19: In the first place, I hear that when you come together as a church, there are divisions among you, and to some extent I believe it. No doubt there have to be differences among you to show which of you have God's approval.

Galatians 5:13-25: You, my brothers and sisters, were called to be free. But do not use your freedom to indulge the flesh; rather, serve one another humbly in love. For the entire law is fulfilled in keeping this one command: "Love your neighbor as yourself." If you bite and devour each other, watch out or you will be destroyed by each other. So I say, walk by the Spirit, and you will not gratify the desires of the flesh. For the flesh desires what is contrary to the Spirit, and the Spirit what is contrary to the flesh. They are in conflict with each other, so that you are not to do whatever you want. But if you are led by the Spirit, you are not under the law. The acts of the flesh are obvious: sexual immorality, impurity and debauchery; idolatry and witchcraft; hatred, discord, jealousy, fits of rage, selfish ambition, dissensions, factions and envy; drunkenness, orgies, and the like. I warn you, as I did before, that those who live like this will not inherit the kingdom of God. But the fruit of the Spirit is love, joy, peace, forbearance, kindness, goodness, faithfulness, gentleness and self-control. Against such things there is no law. Those who belong to Christ Jesus have crucified the flesh with its passions and desires. Since we live by the Spirit, let us keep in step with the Spirit. Let us not become conceited, provoking and envying each other.

James 4:1: What is causing the quarrels and fights among you? Don't they come from the evil desires at war within you?.

Some will argue, and rightfully so, that these verses are addressing different problems, such as, theological heresy, sinful pride, and the contrasting evidence of the fruit of the flesh versus the fruit of the Spirit. However, the main point of all these references is the destructive effects of judging others and the resultant divisions that destroy unity within the church as the body of Christ. D. J. Moo makes the following somber observation:

It is deplorable that the Christian church has so often been characterized by such bitter controversies. The seventeenth-century Jewish philosopher Spinoza observed: "I have often wondered that persons who make the boast of professing the Christian religion—namely love, joy, peace, temperance, and charity to all men—should quarrel with such rancorous animosity and display daily toward one another such bitter hatred, that this, rather than the virtues which they profess, is the readiest criteria of their faith." Some battles are, to be sure, worth fighting; but even then they must be fought without sacrificing Christian principles and virtues. We do not know what the disputes that James refers to were about. At any rate, James seems to be bothered more by the selfish spirit and bitterness of the quarrels than by the rights and wrongs of the various viewpoints.[2]

---

2   D. J. Moo, *James: An Introduction and Commentary,* Vol. 16 (Downers Grove, IL: InterVarsity Press, 1985), 142-143.

Concerning decisions regarding the use of alcohol we cannot help but hear the words of John Calvin echoing in the historical background, referencing some who would create a cult based on these decisions.[3]

> ## Critical Thought
> *Judgment or condemnation of others regarding areas of Christian freedom have no place in the Christian life.*

---

3   Philip Schaff, *History of the Christian Church*, Vol. 7 (Peabody, MA: Hendrickson Publishers, 2011), 53.

Questions for Further Thought

1. On a scale of 1-10, how satisfied are you with the quality of your relationships in general?

2. On a scale of 1-10, how satisfied are you with the quality of your relationships with those you disagree?

3. What needs to change in your heart and mind to improve these relationships?

4. How can you do a better job of displaying the love of Christ, and God's grace and mercy to those with whom you disagree?

5. How do you believe freedom in Christ impacts the decisions you make regarding alcohol use?

8

Learning from Others

"Observe Case Studies of Recovery and Renewal"

Watch and Listen. Understanding the struggles others have with decisions regarding alcohol misuse and addiction emerges from watching and listening to their stories of recovery and renewal with empathy and compassion. Much of this watching and listening occurs in a group setting. Regardless of group type, therapeutic or educational, all share common elements. According to Brook and Spitz, "Any group can act as a setting for an individual to display intense emotions, gain insights, vicariously learn from others, and experience social relatedness and healing effects. All groups aim to increase self-awareness and self-understanding and foster healing experiences."[1]

Listening to the journey of others that range from destruction through recovery, and victory, is one of the primary benefits of both therapeutic groups and recovery groups such as Alcoholics Anonymous,[2] Celebrate Recovery,[3] and Addicts of the Cross.[4] These groups provide a powerful and timely support to those experiencing the predictable challenges that accompany the addiction recovery process. Providing honesty, compassion, a spiritual focus, and systematized steps, recovery groups and their members travel the same path so many others before them have traversed.

---

1   David W. Brook and Henry I. Spitz, *The Group Therapy of Substance Abuse* (New York: The Haworth Medical Press, 2002), 161, 163.

2   Alcoholics Anonymous, *Twelve Steps and Twelve Traditions* (New York: Alcoholics Anonymous World Services, 1981).

3   John Baker, *Celebrate Recovery Leader's Guide* (Grand Rapids, MI: Zondervan, 2012).

4   Larry Skrant, *Addicts at the Cross: A Christian 9-Step Program* (Abbotsford, WI: Aneko Press, 2016).

A common theme of biblically based recovery groups is that "God has a plan and purpose for my life, and that plan is revealed to me through His Holy Word…the Bible is the ultimate guide for laying the groundwork, which will enable a life free of addiction."[5]

Recovery groups, as well as therapeutic groups of all theoretical paradigms, all share a common, foundational task of mutual support and encouragement. Group therapy has been shown to be effective, especially in combination with other treatment modalities (e.g., individual therapy; pharmacotherapy; psychoeducation).[6]

Regarding the mutual support designed into the very foundation of recovery and therapeutic groups, Brown and Lewis note, "AA, Al-Anon, and other 12-step programs are valuable sources of help for people who are facing addiction. Unlike most professional therapies, the 'message' of recovery is carried through an apprentice model. That is, through people who have come before, sharing their reassuring chain of shared experience, individuals learn how to maintain abstinence and build sobriety."[7]

The same may be asserted about therapeutic groups. Mutual support and encouragement is consistently observed and reported by patients as one of the key protective factors and contributors to their successful treatment. The structure of successful, comprehensive treatment is rooted and grounded in an environment of mutual trust and caring. Corey and Corey note:

> The broad purpose of a therapeutic group is to increase people's knowledge of themselves and others, help them clarify the changes they most want to make in their life, and give them some of the tools necessary to make these desired changes. By interacting with others in a trusting and accepting environment, participants are given the opportunity to experiment with novel behavior and to receive honest feedback from others concerning the effects of their behavior.[8]

---

5   Ibid., 1.

6   Frank Minirth, et al., *Taking Control* (Grand Rapids, MI: Baker Books, 1988), 87-88.

7   Stephanie Brown and Virginia Lewis, *The Alcoholic Family in Recovery: A Developmental Model* (New York: The Guilford Press, 1999), 10.

8   Marianne Schneider Corey and Gerald Corey, *Groups Process and Practice* (Pacific Grove, CA: Brooks/Cole Publishing Company, 1992), 9.

This represents a critical function of social support, *especially* within the church. Predictably, alienation, and loneliness accompany the alcohol misuse and addiction recovery process. Relationships that "provide support, caring, and acceptance to someone who is attempting to make a specific behavior change" is critical for the efficacy of recovery groups.[9] Clearly, interpersonal support serves to create a therapeutic environment that catalyzes change.[10] In their discussion of the importance of having an identified support system to the recovery from alcohol dependency, Minirth et al. note, "A support system (like AA) provides help in sharing, caring, overcoming temptation, and direct intervention at the moment of temptation."[11] From the biblical perspective, the value of active support systems, especially as experienced in the group setting, reflects the biblical mandate to relieve others' burdens (Romans 13:9-10).

However, effective recovery groups do more than support abstinence and build sobriety; a fundamental issue confronted is *personal character*. The issue of character is illustrated in a humorous riddle I once heard: "What do you call a drunken horse thief who is in recovery? You call him a sober horse thief." The character-transforming spiritual and moral values emphasized by spiritual recovery program steps, regardless of the therapeutic paradigm, focus on honesty, dependence on a higher power (for biblically based programs, this power is God and the Bible), relational reconciliation and forgiveness, continuous moral self-evaluation, growth, and service to others.[12] The application of recovery steps within most recovery groups is seen as a "spiritual practice."[13]

The mutual encouragement that is a core component of effective recovery groups parallels the primary purpose of Christians meeting

---

9   Velasquez, et al., *Group Treatment for Substance Abuse: A Stages of Change Therapy Manual*, 2nd ed. (New York: The Guilford Press, 2016), 11, 279.

10 Harold S. Bernard and K. Roy McKenzie, eds., *Basics of Group Psychotherapy* (New York: The Guilford Press, 1994), 163.

11 Frank Minirth, et al., *Taking Control* (Grand Rapids, MI: Baker Book House, 1988), 93.

12 Alcoholics Anonymous, *Twelve Steps and Twelve Traditions* (New York: Alcoholics Anonymous World Services, 1981).

13 Rami Shapiro, *Recovery—The Sacred Art: The Twelve Steps as Spiritual Practice* (Woodstock, VT: Skylight Paths Publishing, 2009).

together for worship (Hebrews 10:23-25). According to Urschel, "Support groups provide a safe environment in which you can discover new ways of dealing with your illness, share your triumphs and setbacks with others, exchange information and stories, and gain strength from the knowledge that recovery *is* possible."[14] Judging or condemning those whose lives have disintegrated because of alcohol misuse has no part in the Christian life. Metaphorically, this involves viewing others through a divine lens. This lens is best described with synonymous terms like grace, mercy, forgiveness, and renewal. It is clear that the grace and mercy of God are omnipresent in our lives, including the lives of those enslaved to alcohol misuse. In order to completely experience healing in this regard, we must fully understand the depths of the grace and mercy of God. May calls this "living into grace," and provides these encouraging words:

> In Scripture, nothing portrays our vulnerability to grace more profoundly than the imagery of the desert and the garden. Here, as I have said, Eden represents the garden that is both our birthplace and our destiny, our home and our promised land. Humanity's struggle with addiction is a journey through the wilderness of idolatry where temptations, trials, and deprivations abound, but where God's grace is always available to guide, protect, empower, and transform us.[15]

Many of my patients report their group experience with the following, common responses to this question: "What was the most valuable or impactful part of your group therapy experience?"

- "I did not feel alone. I normally isolated myself when I was abusing alcohol. I never felt isolated in group."

---

14 Harold C. Urschel III, *Healing the Addicted Brain: The Revolutionary Science-Based Alcoholism and Addiction Recovery Program* (Naperville, IL: Sourcebooks, Inc., 2009), 110.

15 Gerald G. May, *Addiction and Grace: Love and Spirituality in the Healing of Addictions* (New York: HarperCollins, 1988), 127, 133.

- "The group encouraged and supported me. Whenever I felt weak, cravings to use again, or even relapse, group members always supported and tried to encourage me through the process."
- "I learned how important honesty is for me and my sobriety. Alcohol abuse turned me into a liar and secret-keeper."
- "I was consistently reminded of the need for me to daily evaluate my moral compass in order to ensure I am still going in the right direction regarding my decisions about alcohol use."
- "I was regularly reminded of the fact we all make decisions we regret. We cannot stay anchored in our past failures but need to look to the future, learn lessons from past failures, and live one day at a time."
- "I learned it is possible to forgive myself and seek forgiveness from those I have harmed."

The essential integration of the social support provided by recovery groups, in combination with a focus on the core component of accompanying character change, is concisely summed up by Minirth with this reminder, "God has given us the power of choice to live our lives to his glory or to ourselves and our own degradation. Choosing to live to his glory also means choosing to keep ourselves healthy in the physical, mental/ emotional, and spiritual areas, body, soul, and spirit, of our lives."[16]"[16]

It is essential for us to *watch and listen* to the struggles of those trying to traverse the difficult terrain of recovery from alcohol misuse while, simultaneously, providing the encouragement, support, and understanding that serve as pillars of the successful recovery process.

> **Critical Thought**
> *Observe and listen to recovery stories of others in order to gain wisdom regarding alcohol-use decisions.*

---

16 Frank Minirth, et al., *Taking Control* (Grand Rapids, MI: Baker Book House, 1988), 97.

Questions for Further Thought

1. *Would you ever consider attending a recovery group like Alcoholics Anonymous or Celebrate Recovery?*

2. *If you have never considered attending a recovery group, why not?*

3. *If you have ever thought about attending a recovery group, but currently are not, what is preventing you from attending regularly?*

4. *What emotions do you feel when you meet someone in recovery, or hear their story of recovery from alcohol misuse?*

5. *What do you believe is the relationship between the human condition, God's grace, mercy, and forgiveness, and your attitude toward those struggling with recovery from alcohol misuse?*

9

—ɯɯ—

Conclusion

"Now What?"

Decision Time. Since before recorded time, natural processes have created alcohol in the form of fermenting, rotting fruit, that has fallen to the ground. Animals have eaten this fermented fruit and become "staggeringly drunk."[1] Today this process has been documented many times by observers of animal behavior. Humans are not immune from this behavior. Beginning with the use of alcohol-laden, rotting fruit, the manufacture of alcoholic beverages has progressed, including the introduction of the distillation process, a human-manufactured process of increased alcohol content in these beverages.

Accompanying this ever-present alcohol throughout history has been over-use, known today as alcohol abuse. Alcohol abuse results in a predictable pattern of dysfunctional thinking and destructive behavior, leading to the erosion of all life domains, whether health, relationships, finances, career, spiritual life, and, sometimes, accompanying legal problems.[2] Without an understanding of the evidence-based line of demarcation between alcohol use and abuse, guesswork (What is my limit?) and hope ("I hope I don't drink too much tonight.") provide unsteady and untrustworthy guidance for the alcohol-user.

This uncertainty will lead to violation of the biblical command to "be not drunk with wine, which is in excess, but be filled with the Holy Spirit."

---

1   Darryl S. Inaba and William E. Cohen, *Uppers, Downers, All-Arounders: Physical and Mental Effects of Psychoactive Drugs* (Medford, OR: CNS Publications, 2011), 5.2.

2   *Diagnostic and Statistical Manual of Mental Disorders,* 5th ed. (Washington, DC: American Psychiatric Publishing, 2013), 492.

(Ephesians 5:18). This poses a very real challenge for the Christian who uses alcohol.[3] Initial evidence indicates that up to 10 percent of Christians may currently suffer from alcohol-use disorders. Recent evidence reveals that as many as 119 million Americans use alcohol, while alcohol abuse is the number one cause of preventable death in the United States. Alcohol abusers (including Christians) tend to engage in denial or secrecy regarding this behavior.[4] The primary question the Bible presents us with is this: "Who or what is controlling my life?"

For Christians, the question, "Now what?" logically follows after reading a book like this. Taking action or living intentionally, is the clearest message the Bible has for all of us. Living my life in such a way that I *intentionally* focus on balanced living that reflects God's comprehensive truth, from both the Bible and nature, must be the primary goal in life for all Christians. Emerging out of the concept of intentional living is what Koch and Haugk refer to as "assertive living." They note:

> Assertive behavior is integral and essential to the Christian lifestyle. Assertive behavior is behavior that honors the self while honoring others. The assertive person authentically cares for others and at the same time engages in God-pleasing self-care. Individuals who think and behave assertively are people who have an active orientation to life, people who participate fully in life, people that a sense of Godgiven personal power… Assertive men and women live decisively, aware that life is full of choices and are sensitive to their responsibility to make decisions about those choices…Not only are you able to make choices about your thinking, you can also make choices about your behavior. The most visible evidence that you are behaving in a responsible manner is that you can actually choose behaviors that give evidence of your faith life and that are an outward sign of your assertive thinking.[5]

---

3   Ibid, 493.

4   Tim Clinton and Eric Scalise, *Addictions and Recovery Counseling* (Grand Rapids, MI: Baker Books, 2013), 70-71.

5   Ruth N. Koch and Kenneth C. Haugk, *Speaking the Truth in Love: How to Be an Assertive Christian* (St. Louis, MO: Stephen Ministries, 1992), 23, 26, 34.

While it is true the goal of assertive, intentional living is comprised of many different tasks, the glory of God represents the intended, overarching directional azimuth and desired end-state of our lives (First Corinthians 10:31).

In conclusion, there are seven specific, critical spiritual tasks suggested here. The following list summarizes these critical tasks and lessons learned emerging out of this book:

1. Psychoeducation regarding medical facts surrounding alcohol use, and the onset and development of alcohol use disorders, provides invaluable insight into decisions by Christians regarding alcohol use. Understanding the onset and progression of alcohol-use disorders that result from alcohol abuse will provide critical insight, leading to wise decisions concerning alcohol use. This task may be viewed within the context of the discipleship process. Integrating biblical and natural truth into my life in such a way that results in emotional and spiritual growth is a key component of the all-encompassing task of personal psychoeducation and discipleship.

2. Discipleship that explores the comprehensive biblical teaching about alcohol use and abuse provides significant spiritual growth opportunities, enabling wise decisions in connection with alcohol use. Wisdom, the application of truth to my life, the ground from which personal protection, insight, and growth occurs, is the target for which Christians must aim. Solomon reminds us of this in the book of Proverbs when he writes, "Do not forsake wisdom, and she will protect you; love her, and she will watch over you. The beginning of wisdom is this: Get wisdom. Though it cost all you have, get understanding" (Proverbs 4:6-7).

The power of applied biblical teaching to one's life not only provides wisdom but results in corrective doctrine for training in righteousness (Second Timothy 3:16). This training includes wise decisions involving alcohol use. Wisdom in the area of alcohol use provides leverage for living the abundant Christian life.

3. Alcohol abuse over time leads to the destruction of all areas of life. The progressively destructive effects of alcohol abuse over time represents a complex web of deterioration in all life domains. The diagnostic criteria defining alcohol abuse view all life domains in making a medical determination of alcohol use disorders. These life domains include health,

relationships, financial, career, spiritual, and legal. Alcohol abuse will, given enough time, negatively affect most or all of these areas of life.

4.   Alcohol abuse slowly erodes the moral decision-making power of the believer. Over time, alcohol abuse slowly disrupts the ability to not only *know* the difference between biblical and moral right and wrong, but also the *ability* to make wise decisions regarding alcohol use. Alcohol abuse will-not might-skew the believer's moral compass until it becomes diametrically opposed to the moral will of God for the life of the Christian.

5.   Decisions regarding alcohol use is an issue that must be actively engaged with by all believers and spiritual leaders. This issue cannot be ignored, *especially* for those in a position of spiritual leadership. Scripture is clear in this regard; spiritual leaders must be above reproach, including in the area of alcohol misuse (First Timothy 3:1-14).

6.   God's grace and freedom in Christ allow for individual believer's alcohol-use decisions that will not lead to abuse. Biblically, alcohol use is allowed, while alcohol abuse is clearly condemned as an egregious sin (see Appendix 1; Proverbs 23:29-34; Romans 13:13-14; Galatians 5:19-24). This point poses a clear challenge for Christians because there is a fine line between living within the grace of God and our freedom in Christ, versus going too far, leading us into sin. The apostle Paul references this when he warns us to not use our freedom in Christ as a license to sin. He writes, "You, my brothers and sisters, were called to be free. But do not use your freedom to indulge the flesh; rather, serve one another humbly in love. For the entire law is fulfilled in keeping this one command: 'Love your neighbor as yourself'" (Galatians 5:13-14).

A proper understanding and application of the grace of God and our freedom in Christ to all areas of our lives, including alcohol-use decisions, will allow us to fulfill part of our calling ("serve one another humbly in love") and avoid "indulging the flesh" (sinning).

7.   God's grace and freedom in Christ mitigates against judging others who have a different conviction regarding abstinence versus moderation in alcohol use (Matthew 7:1-5; Romans 14:1-13; Titus 3:2-7). Throughout the history of the church it is clear that Christians have held to differing views regarding alcohol use. Hence, the need for biblical clarification of this potentially destructive issue. While alcohol abuse is specifically condemned,

the Bible allows for alcohol use.[6] Those who differ on abstinence versus moderation of alcohol use must not engage in judgment or condemnation of the other. The decision to engage or not engage in non-abusive alcohol use represents freedom in Christ (Galatians 5:1, 13-14).

It is incumbent on all believers to understand the aggregate spectrum of God's truth, and integrate and apply this understanding to life decisions regarding alcohol use, in order to create and maintain a vital spiritual life with God. This spiritual life must be characterized by proper moral decision-making involved with the assessment to use or abstain from alcohol, in combination with a committed, non-judgmental attitude toward others who may disagree with my position. The Bible presents clear wisdom, commands, and prohibitions regarding decisions about alcohol use. It also presents biblical guidance for application of *intentionality* to living the Christian life and transformation that emerges out of the renewed mind. Challies makes this insightful observation:

We use discernment, then, to distinguish between what is good and what is bad. We learn what God would have us do in a given situation by looking to the truths of the Bible and separating the options before us that are bad from the ones that are good. We use discernment to apply the truth of the Bible to the situations we face in daily life. Through discerning God's will we make decisions and act in ways that are shaped by what we believe to be true about God. We make decisions that honor him and bring glory to his holy name.[7]

The following biblical guidance and accompanying actions are unequivocal in this regard (all verses from the NASB):

Romans 12:2: "And do not be conformed to this world, but be transformed by the renewing of your mind, so that you may prove what the will of God is, that which is good and acceptable and perfect."

---

6   "Wine, Alcohol in the Bible," *BibleStudy.Org*, Accessed January 3, 2019, http://www.biblestudy.org/bible-study-by-topic/proverbs/alcohol-wine.html.

7   Tim Challies, *The Discipline of Spiritual Discernment* (Wheaton, IL: Crossway, 2007), 121.

Psalm 51:10: "Create in me a clean heart, O God, and renew a steadfast spirit within me."

Ezekiel 18:31: "Cast away from you all your transgressions which you have committed and make yourselves a new heart and a new spirit. For why will you die, O house of Israel?"

Ezekiel 36:26: "Moreover, I will give you a new heart and put a new spirit within you; and I will remove the heart of stone from your flesh and give you a heart of flesh."

Second Corinthians 5:17: "Therefore if anyone is in Christ, he is a new creature; the old things passed away; behold, new things have come."

Ephesians 4:22-24: "…that, in reference to your former manner of life, you lay aside the old self, which is being corrupted in accordance with the lusts of deceit, and that you be renewed in the spirit of your mind, and put on the new self, which in the likeness of God has been created in righteousness and holiness of the truth."

Colossians 1:21-22: "And although you were formerly alienated and hostile in mind, engaged in evil deeds, yet He has now reconciled you in His fleshly body through death, in order to present you before Him holy and blameless and beyond reproach—"

Titus 3:5: "He saved us, not on the basis of deeds which we have done in righteousness, but according to His mercy, by the washing of regeneration and renewing by the Holy Spirit."

Solomon encourages the reader with these words: "Let the wise listen to these proverbs and become even wiser. Let those with understanding receive guidance by exploring the meaning in these proverbs and parables, the words of the wise and their riddles. Fear of the Lord is the foundation of true knowledge, but fools despise wisdom and discipline" (Proverbs 1:5-7).

A final encouragement for Christians in view of the second coming of Christ and the work of God in the world and in our lives is found in First Thessalonians 5:1-11:

Now, brothers and sisters, about times and dates we do not need to write to you, for you know very well that the day of the Lord will come like a thief in the night. While people are saying, "Peace and safety," destruction will come on them suddenly, as labor pains on a pregnant woman, and they will not escape. But you, brothers and sisters, are not in darkness so that this day should surprise you like a thief. You are all children of the light and children of the day. We do not belong to the night or to the darkness. So then, let us not be like others, who are asleep, but let us be awake and sober. For those who sleep, sleep at night, and those who get drunk, get drunk at night. But since we belong to the day, let us be sober, putting on faith and love as a breastplate, and the hope of salvation as a helmet. For God did not appoint us to suff r wrath but to receive salvation through our Lord Jesus Christ. He died for us so that, whether we are awake or asleep, we may live together with him. Therefore encourage one another and build each other up, just as in fact you are doing).

Living intentionally represents a core spiritual task function for all Christians, and is a fundamental biblical principle that also reflects Homer's idea of precommitment when dealing with the Siren's songs in *Odysseus*, his classic work from Greek mythology. But the Bible is not based on mythology; it is the eternal, infallible, Word of God presenting us with the authoritative divine guidance for all areas of life. This is especially true regarding alcohol-use decisions. David Jeremiah makes the following comments regarding the clear connection between sanctified intentional living and the second coming of Christ:

Since Christ may come at any moment we should live productively, faithfully, and expectantly....The second coming shouldn't provoke idleness among believers, but action; not speculation, but sanctification....Therefore, beloved, looking forward to these things, be diligent to be found by Him in peace, without spot and blameless....While awaiting our Lord's return, we must stand on His great and precious promises, which provide all we need for life and godliness.[8]

Complementary biblically based principles that contribute to spiritual success include an exact understanding of biblical teaching about alcohol use, appropriate application of the grace of God to life, a factual and truth-based view of alcohol use, and an overarching commitment to obedience to God's Word. For the believer, it is imperative to living intentionally, seeking God's best in all of our decisions. Establishing the critical objective, quantifiable, evidence-based boundary to alcohol use will protect us from trespassing into the territory of alcohol abuse and being guilty of the biblical condemnation of this deprecating sin.

The foundational cornerstone of this book is Christ Himself. Without an accurate and heart-changing vision of the good news of His work and vision of His glory that must embed your heart on a daily basis, this book is useless. The good news of Christ, His actual atoning death as payment for our sins, His literal, physical resurrection from the dead, and His ascension into heaven with the accompanying promise of His return, is the basis of our forgiveness, transformation, new life, and hope in a hopeless world or situation (see First Corinthians 15).

All glory is due Him as creator of all things, the lamb slain before the foundation of the world (First Peter 1:19-20; Revelation 13:8), and seated at the right hand of the Father (Hebrews 1:11-14; Revelation 3:21), where He is the recipient of the eternal proclamation of "Holy, holy, holy is the Lord almighty" (Isaiah 6:3). This personal knowledge of Jesus Christ residing in a repentant heart is the necessary ground upon which all motivation and decisions in life are rooted and grounded. Without first coming to Christ by faith, the specific battle surrounding alcohol use cannot be won. As a matter of fact, *all* is lost apart from Christ. In Philippians 3:3-10, the apostle Paul makes this point when he challenges us with these words:

For it is we who are the circumcision, we who serve God by his Spirit, who boast in Christ Jesus, and who put no confidence in

---

8   David Jeremiah, *Understanding the Books of the Bible* (San Diego, CA: Turning Point, 2014), 225, 229, 261.

the flesh— though I myself have reasons for such confidence. If someone else thinks they have reasons to put confidence in the flesh, I have more: circumcised on the eighth day, of the people of Israel, of the tribe of Benjamin, a Hebrew of Hebrews; in regard to the law, a Pharisee; as for zeal, persecuting the church; as for righteousness based on the law, faultless. But whatever were gains to me I now consider loss for the sake of Christ. What is more, I consider everything a loss because of the surpassing worth of knowing Christ Jesus my Lord, for whose sake I have lost all things. I consider them garbage, that I may gain Christ and be found in him, not having a righteousness of my own that comes from the law, but that which is through faith in Christ— the righteousness that comes from God on the basis of faith. I want to know Christ— yes, to know the power of his resurrection and participation in his sufferings, becoming like him in his death (NIV).

Paul's point? Without a personal knowledge of, and commitment to, the gospel of Christ and vision of His glory, *I am lost.* Coming to Christ through faith, repentance, and receiving Him as Savior and Lord, is the first step to victory over the temptations and sin in my life (John 1:12; 3:5; Romans 10:910). In Philippians 3:10, Paul references his former life of rigid religious accommodation and apparent moral exactitude that was seemingly above reproach. Yet, he recounts his experience with the risen Christ that led to his transformation and reconciliation with the very God he was persecuting. He describes this exchange of his faux truth with the eternal truth of the good news and necessity of Christ's work on the cross as "counting it all (his previous religious morality) as "garbage" for the sake of knowing Christ *personally.*

Melick explains: "Paul said he counted all things as loss 'that I might gain Christ' (Philippians 3:8). Here Paul clearly developed the idea of exchange. It was impossible to hold on to the former values and still have Christ. It was one or the other, and Christ exceeded anything and everything else. The three statements express repentance regarding Paul's former attitudes about salvation. He turned away from the past to gain Christ".[9]

---

9   R. R. Melick, *Philippians, Colossians, Philemon*, Vol. 32 (Nashville: Broadman & Holman Publishers, 1991), 132.

This book closes with the incisive words of Dr. John MacArthur from his monumental work on Isaiah 53, *The Gospel According to God*: "The atonement accomplished through the suffering of Yahweh's servant is the necessary ground and prerequisite for every other expression of God's grace and deliverance."[10] What have you done with this truth? What have you done with Christ? How are you approaching the Christian life, *especially* regarding decisions surrounding alcohol use?

God's grace is a wonderful truth, but carries with it the warning against alcohol abuse. We must never misappropriate this grace and our freedom in Christ to justify sin (Galatians 5:1, 13-14). God's expectation for His children has never changed; "Be holy, because I am holy" (First Peter 1:16).

"Dear God, may I grow in the
grace and knowledge of my Lord
and Savior, Jesus Christ."[11]

"So whether you eat or drink, or whatever you
do, do it all for the glory of God"

First Corinthians 10:31

---

10   John MacArthur, *The Gospel According to God* (Wheaton, IL: Crossway Books, 2018), 190.
11   David Jeremiah, *Understanding the Books of the Bible* (San Diego, CA: Turning Point, 2014), 261.

10

—⟋⟍—

Appendices

Appendix 1: Alcohol-Related Bible Verses

Accepted as normal

Genesis 14:18: "And Melchizedek, the king of Salem and a priest of God Most High, brought Abram some bread and wine."

Genesis 27:25: "Then Isaac said, 'Now, my son, bring me the wild game. Let me eat it, and then I will give you my blessing.' So Jacob took the food to his father, and Isaac ate it. He also drank the wine that Jacob served him."

Deuteronomy 14:24-26: "Now when the Lord your God blesses you with a good harvest, the place of worship he chooses for his name to be honored might be too far for you to bring the tithe. If so, you may sell the tithe portion of your crops and herds, put the money in a pouch, and go to the place the Lord your God has chosen. When you arrive, you may use the money to buy any kind of food you want—cattle, sheep, goats, wine, or other alcoholic drink. Then feast there in the presence of the Lord your God and celebrate with your household."

Judges 9:13: "But the grapevine also refused, saying, 'Should I quit producing the wine that cheers both God and people, just to wave back and forth over the trees?'"

Psalm 104:14-15: "You cause grass to grow for the livestock and plants for people to use. You allow them to produce food from the earth—wine to make them glad, olive oil to soothe their skin, and bread to give them strength."

Ecclesiastes 8:15: "So I recommend having fun, because there is nothing better for people in this world than to eat, drink, and enjoy life. That way they will experience some happiness along with all the hard work God gives them under the sun."

Matthew 11:18-19: "For John didn't spend his time eating and drinking, and you say, 'He's possessed by a demon.' The Son of Man, on the other hand, feasts and drinks, and you say, 'He's a glutton and a drunkard, and a friend of tax collectors and other sinners.' But wisdom is shown to be right by its results."

Matthew 26:26-30: "As they were eating, Jesus took some bread and blessed it. Then he broke it in pieces and gave it to the disciples, saying, 'Take this and eat it, for this is my body.' And he took a cup of wine and gave thanks to God for it. He gave it to them and said, 'Each of you drink from it, for this is my blood, which confirms the covenant between God and his people. It is poured out as a sacrifice to forgive the sins of many. Mark my words—I will not drink wine again until the day I drink it new with you in my Father's Kingdom.' Then they sang a hymn and went out to the Mount of Olives."

Mark 14:25: "I tell you the truth, I will not drink wine again until the day I drink it new in the Kingdom of God."

John 2:7-11: "Jesus told the servants, 'Fill the jars with water'. When the jars had been filled, he said, 'Now dip some out, and take it to the master of ceremonies.' So the servants followed his instructions. When the master of ceremonies tasted the water that was now wine, not knowing where it had come from (though, of course, the servants knew), he called the bridegroom over. 'A host always serves the best wine first,' he said. 'Then, when everyone has had a lot to drink, he brings out the less expensive wine. But you have kept the best until now.' This miraculous sign at Cana in Galilee was the first time Jesus revealed his glory. And his disciples believed in him."

First Corinthians 6:12: "You say, 'I am allowed to do anything'—but not everything is good for you. And even though 'I am allowed to do anything,' I must not become a slave to anything."

First Timothy 5:22-23: "Never be in a hurry about appointing a church leader. Do not share in the sins of others. Keep yourself pure. Don't drink only water. You ought to drink a little wine for the sake of your stomach because you are sick so often."

As a blessing from God

Genesis 27:28: "From the dew of heaven and the richness of the earth, may God always give you abundant harvests of grain and bountiful new wine."

Genesis 27:37: "Isaac said to Esau, 'I have made Jacob your master and have declared that all his brothers will be his servants. I have guaranteed him an abundance of grain and wine—what is left for me to give you, my son?'"

Second Chronicles 2:10: "In payment for your woodcutters, I will send 100,000 bushels of crushed wheat, 100,000 bushels of barley, 110,000 gallons of wine, and 110,000 gallons of olive oil."

Isaiah 62:8-9: "The Lord has sworn to Jerusalem by his own strength: 'I will never again hand you over to your enemies. Never again will foreign warriors come and take away your grain and new wine. You raised the grain, and you will eat it, praising the Lord. Within the courtyards of the Temple, you yourselves will drink the wine you have pressed.'"

Ecclesiastes 9:7: "So go ahead. Eat your food with joy, and drink your wine with a happy heart, for God approves of this."

Jeremiah 31:12: "They will come home and sing songs of joy on the heights of Jerusalem. They will be radiant because of the Lord's good gifts—the abundant crops of grain, new wine, and olive oil, and the healthy flocks and herds. Their life will be like a watered garden, and all their sorrows will be gone."

Joel 2:24-25: "The threshing floors will again be piled high with grain, and the presses will overflow with new wine and olive oil. The Lord says, 'I will give you back what you lost to the swarming locusts, the hopping locusts, the stripping locusts, and the cutting locusts. It was I who sent this great destroying army against you.'"

Amos 9:14: "I will bring my exiled people of Israel back from distant lands, and they will rebuild their ruined cities and live in them again. They will plant vineyards and gardens; they will eat their crops and drink their wine."

Nehemiah 8:10: "And Nehemiah continued, 'Go and celebrate with a feast of rich foods and sweet drinks, and share gifts of food with people who have nothing prepared. This is a sacred day before our Lord. Don't be dejected and sad, for the joy of the Lord is your strength.'"

As an offering to God

Exodus 29:40: "With one of them, offer two quarts of choice flour mixed with one quart of pure oil of pressed olives; also, offer one quart of wine as a liquid offering. "

Leviticus 23:13: "With it you must present a grain offering consisting of four quarts of choice flour moistened with olive oil. It will be a special gift, a pleasing aroma to the Lord. You must also offer one quart of wine as a liquid offering."

Numbers 6:20: "Then the priest will lift them up as a special offering before the Lord. These are holy portions for the priest, along with the breast of the special offering and the thigh of the sacred offering that are lifted up before the Lord. After this ceremony the Nazirites may again drink wine."

Numbers 15:5: "For each lamb offered as a burnt offering or a special sacrifice, you must also present one quart of wine as a liquid offering."

First Corinthians 10:31: "So whether you eat or drink, or whatever you do, do it all for the glory of God."

Alcohol Abuse

Ephesians 5:18 "Don't be drunk with wine, because that will ruin your life. Instead, be filled with the Holy Spirit."

Galatians 5:19-26: "When you follow the desires of your sinful nature, the results are very clear: sexual immorality, impurity, lustful pleasures, idolatry, sorcery, hostility, quarreling, jealousy, outbursts of anger, selfish ambition, dissension, division, envy, drunkenness, wild parties, and other sins like these. Let me tell you again, as I have before, that anyone living that sort of life will not inherit the Kingdom of God. But the Holy Spirit produces this kind of fruit in our lives: love, joy, peace, patience, kindness, goodness, faithfulness, gentleness, and self-control. There is no law against these things. Those who belong to Christ Jesus have nailed the passions and desires of their sinful nature to his cross and crucified them there. Since we are living by the Spirit, let us follow the Spirit's leading in every part of our lives. Let us not become conceited, or provoke one another, or be jealous of one another."

Condemned

Isaiah 28:1: "What sorrow awaits the proud city of Samaria—the glorious crown of the drunks of Israel. It sits at the head of a fertile valley, but its glorious beauty will fade like a flower. It is the pride of a people brought down by wine."

Galatians 5:19-21: "When you follow the desires of your sinful nature, the results are very clear: sexual immorality, impurity, lustful pleasures, idolatry, sorcery, hostility, quarreling, jealousy, outbursts of anger, selfish ambition, dissension, division, envy, drunkenness, wild parties, and other sins like these. Let me tell you again, as I have before, that anyone living that sort of life will not inherit the Kingdom of God."

Is a curse on humanity

Lamentations 4:21-22: "Are you rejoicing in the land of Uz, O people of Edom? But you, too, must drink from the cup of the Lord's anger. You, too, will be stripped naked in your drunkenness. O beautiful Jerusalem, your punishment will end; you will soon return from exile. But Edom, your punishment is just beginning; soon your many sins will be exposed."

Habakkuk 2:15-16: "What sorrow awaits you who make your neighbors drunk. You force your cup on them so you can gloat over their shameful nakedness. But soon it will be your turn to be disgraced. Come, drink and be exposed. Drink from the cup of the Lord's judgment, and all your glory will be turned to shame."

Causes cognitive distortions

Proverbs 23:29-35: "Who has anguish? Who has sorrow? Who is always fighting? Who is always complaining? Who has unnecessary bruises? Who has bloodshot eyes? It is the one who spends long hours in the taverns, trying out new drinks. Don't gaze at the wine, seeing how red it is, how it sparkles in the cup, how smoothly it goes down. For in the end it bites like a poisonous snake; it stings like a viper. You will see hallucinations, and you will say crazy things. You will stagger like a sailor tossed at sea, clinging to a swaying mast. And you will say, 'They hit me, but I didn't feel it. I didn't even know it when they beat me up. When will I wake up so I can look for another drink?'"

Isaiah 28:7: "Now, however, Israel is led by drunks. who reel with wine and stagger with alcohol. The priests and prophets stagger with alcohol and lose themselves in wine. They reel when they see visions and stagger as they render decisions.

Deteriorates job performance

Proverbs 23:20-21: "Do not carouse with drunkards or feast with gluttons, for they are on their way to poverty, and too much sleep clothes them in rags. "

Proverbs 31:4-5-: "It is not for kings, O Lemuel, to guzzle wine. Rulers should not crave alcohol. For if they drink, they may forget the law and not give justice to the oppressed. "

Destroys relationships

Proverbs 23:29: "Who has anguish? Who has sorrow? Who is always fighting? Who is always complaining? Who has unnecessary bruises? Who has bloodshot eyes?"

Erodes health

Proverbs 23:30-32: "Don't be the one who spends long hours in the taverns, trying out new drinks. Don't gaze at the wine, seeing how red it is, how it sparkles in the cup, how smoothly it goes down. For in the end it bites like a poisonous snake; it stings like a viper."

Hosea 7:5: "On royal holidays, the princes get drunk with wine, carousing with those who mock them."

Deteriorates morals

Genesis 9:21: "One day he drank some wine he had made, and he became drunk and lay naked inside his tent."

Habakkuk 2:5: "Furthermore, wine betrays the haughty man, so that he does not stay at home. He enlarges his appetite like Sheol, and he is like death, never satisfied. He also gathers to himself all nations and collects to himself all peoples."

Disqualifies from church leadership

First Timothy 3:1-3: "This is a trustworthy saying: 'If someone aspires to be a church leader, he desires an honorable position.' So a church leader must be a man whose life is above reproach. He must be faithful to his wife. He must exercise self-control, live wisely, and have a good reputation. He must enjoy having guests in his home, and he must be able to teach. He must not be a heavy drinker or be violent. He must be gentle, not quarrelsome, and not love money."

Titus 2:3: "Similarly, teach the older women to live in a way that honors God. They must not slander others or be heavy drinkers. Instead, they should teach others what is good. "

Appendix 2: Spiritual Maturity-Related Bible Verses

Psalm 92:12-14 "But the godly will flourish like palm trees and grow strong like the cedars of Lebanon. For they are transplanted to the Lord's own house. They flourish in the courts of our God. Even in old age they will still produce fruit; they will remain vital and green."

Proverbs 1:1-5: "These are the proverbs of Solomon, David's son, king of Israel. Their purpose is to teach people wisdom and discipline, to help them understand the insights of the wise. Their purpose is to teach people to live disciplined and successful lives, to help them do what is right, just, and fair. These proverbs will give insight to the simple, knowledge and discernment to the young. Let the wise listen to these proverbs and become even wiser. Let those with understanding receive guidance"

Luke 2:52: "Jesus grew in wisdom and in stature and in favor with God and all the people."

Luke 8:14-15: "The seeds that fell among the thorns represent those who hear the message, but all too quickly the message is crowded out by the cares and riches and pleasures of this life. And so they never grow into maturity. And the seeds that fell on the good soil represent honest, good-hearted people who hear God's word, cling to it, and patiently produce a huge harvest."

First Corinthians 2:6: "Yet when I am among mature believers, I do speak with words of wisdom, but not the kind of wisdom that belongs to this world or to the rulers of this world, who are soon forgotten."

First Corinthians 3:1-3: "Dear brothers and sisters, when I was with you I couldn't talk to you as I would to spiritual people. I had to talk as though you belonged to this world or as though you were infants in Christ. I had to feed you with milk, not with solid food, because you weren't ready for anything stronger. And you still aren't ready, for you are still controlled by your sinful nature."

First Corinthians 13:11: "When I was a child, I spoke and thought and reasoned as a child. But when I grew up, I put away childish things."

First Corinthians 14:20: "Dear brothers and sisters, don't be childish in your understanding of these things. Be innocent as babies when it comes to evil but be mature in understanding matters of this kind."

Ephesians 4:13: "This will continue until we all come to such unity in our faith and knowledge of God's Son that we will be mature in the Lord, measuring up to the full and complete standard of Christ."

Ephesians 4:20-24: "But that isn't what you learned about Christ. Since you have heard about Jesus and have learned the truth that comes from him, throw off your old sinful nature and your former way of life, which is corrupted by lust and deception. Instead, let the Spirit renew your thoughts and attitudes. Put on your new nature, created to be like God—truly righteous and holy."

Philippians 3:13-16: "No, dear brothers and sisters, I have not achieved it, but I focus on this one thing: Forgetting the past and looking forward to what lies ahead, I press on to reach the end of the race and receive the heavenly prize for which God, through Christ Jesus, is calling us. Let all who are spiritually mature agree on these things. If you disagree on some point, I believe God will make it plain to you. But we must hold on to the progress we have already made."

Colossians 1:9-10: "So we have not stopped praying for you since we first heard about you. We ask God to give you complete knowledge of his will and to give you spiritual wisdom and understanding. Then the way you live will always honor and please the Lord, and your lives will produce every kind of good fruit. All the while, you will grow as you learn to know God better and better."

Colossians 1:28: "So we tell others about Christ, warning everyone and teaching everyone with all the wisdom God has given us. We want to present them to God, perfect in their relationship to Christ."

Colossians 2:6-7: "And now, just as you accepted Christ Jesus as your Lord, you must continue to follow him. Let your roots grow down into him, and let your lives be built on him. Then your faith will grow strong in the truth you were taught, and you will overflow with thankfulness."

Colossians 3:9-10: "Don't lie to each other, for you have stripped off your old sinful nature and all its wicked deeds. Put on your new nature and be renewed as you learn to know your Creator and become like him."

Second Timothy 3:16-17: "All Scripture is inspired by God and is useful to teach us what is true and to make us realize what is wrong in our lives. It corrects us when we are wrong and teaches us to do what is right. God uses it to prepare and equip his people to do every good work."

Hebrews 5:12-14: "You have been believers so long now that you ought to be teaching others. Instead, you need someone to teach you again the basic things about God's word. You are like babies who need milk and cannot eat solid food. For someone who lives on milk is still an infant and doesn't know how to do what is right. Solid food is for those who are mature, who through training have the skill to recognize the difference between right and wrong."

Hebrews 6:1: "So let us stop going over the basic teachings about Christ again and again. Let us go on instead and become mature in our understanding. Surely we don't need to start again with the fundamental importance of repenting from evil deeds and placing our faith in God."

First Peter 2:2-3: "Like newborn babies, you must crave pure spiritual milk so that you will grow into a full experience of salvation. Cry out for this nourishment, now that you have had a taste of the Lord's kindness."

Second Peter 1:2: "May God give you more and more grace and peace as you grow in your knowledge of God and Jesus our Lord."

Second Peter 1:10: "So, dear brothers and sisters, work hard to prove that you really are among those God has called and chosen. Do these things, and you will never fall away."

Second Peter 2:20: "And when people escape from the wickedness of the world by knowing our Lord and Savior Jesus Christ and then get tangled up and enslaved by sin again, they are worse off than before."

Second Peter 3:18: "Rather, you must grow in the grace and knowledge of our Lord and Savior Jesus Christ. All glory to him, both now and forever. Amen."

Revelation 1:6: "He has made us a Kingdom of priests for God his Father. All glory and power to him forever and ever. Amen."

Appendix 3: The Will of God Bible Verses (NIV)

Psalm 40:8: "I desire to do your will, my God; your law is within my heart."

Psalm 135:6: "The Lord does whatever pleases him, in the heavens and on the earth, in the seas and all their depths."

Matthew 6:10: "Your kingdom come, your will be done, on earth as it is in heaven."

Matthew 12:50: "For whoever does the will of my Father in heaven is my brother and sister and mother."

Matthew 26:39: "Going a little farther, he fell with his face to the ground and prayed, 'My Father, if it is possible, may this cup be taken from me. Yet not as I will, but as you will.'"

Luke 22:42: "Father, if you are willing, take this cup from me; yet not my will, but yours be done."

John 4:34: "My food," said Jesus, "is to do the will of him who sent me and to finish his work."

John 7:16–17: "Jesus answered, 'My teaching is not my own. It comes from the one who sent me. Anyone who chooses to do the will of God will find out whether my teaching comes from God or whether I speak on my own.'"

Acts 2:23: "This man was handed over to you by God's deliberate plan and foreknowledge; and you, with the help of wicked men, put him to death by nailing him to the cross."

Romans 12:1–2: "Therefore, I urge you, brothers and sisters, in view of God's mercy, to offer your bodies as a living sacrifice, holy and pleasing to God—this is your true and proper worship. Do not conform to the pattern of this world, but be transformed by the renewing of your mind. Then you will be able to test and approve what God's will is— his good, pleasing and perfect will."

Romans 15:32: "…so that I may come to you with joy, by God's will, and in your company be refreshed."

Ephesians 1:4–11: "For he chose us in him before the creation of the world to be holy and blameless in his sight. In love he predestined us for adoption to sonship through Jesus Christ, in accordance with his pleasure and will—to the praise of his glorious grace, which he has freely given us in the One he loves. In him we have redemption through his blood, the forgiveness of sins, in accordance with the riches of God's grace of his will according to his good pleasure, which he purposed in Christ, to be put into effect when the times reach their fulfillment—to bring unity to all things in heaven and on earth under Christ. In him we were also chosen, having been predestined according to the plan of him who works out everything in conformity with the purpose of his will."

Colossians 1:9: "For this reason, since the day we heard about you, we have not stopped praying for you. We continually ask God to fill you with the knowledge of his will through all the wisdom and understanding that the Spirit gives."

11

—m—

Index of Scriptures and Subjects

A

AA 7, 57, 60, 146, 147

Abstinence 5, 26, 104, 105, 106, 187, 188, 189

Acts 46, 86, 93, 174

Acts 10:43 93

Acts 23:1 86

Alcohol Abuse 51, 52, 113, 117, 167, 186, 190

Alcohol abuse as a curse on humanity 101

Alcohol abuse causes cognitive distortions 101

Alcohol abuse condemned 101

Alcohol abuse destroys relationships 102

Alcohol abuse deteriorates morals 103

Alcohol abuse disqualifies from church leadership 103

Alcohol abuse erodes health 102

Alcohol as an offering to God 5, 99

Alcoholics Anonymous 7, 57, 58, 60, 110, 120, 145, 147, 151, 181

alcohol misuse 11, 15, 23, 24, 28, 46, 50, 51, 52, 53, 54, 56, 63, 103, 107, 145, 147, 148, 150, 151, 156

alcohol production 22, 23

Alcohol use as a blessing from God 5, 97

Alcohol Use Disorder 56, 110

American Society of Addiction Medicine 7, 57, 66, 73, 189

Amos 98, 166

Animals 23, 153

APA 7, 43

aphorism 103

AUD 7, 56, 74

B

Bible 4, 6, 7, 17, 20, 22, 24, 25, 28, 30, 31, 33, 34, 35, 36, 39, 40, 41, 42, 43, 44, 45, 46, 47, 54, 59, 62, 63, 66, 67, 68, 69, 71, 72, 81, 82, 83, 84, 85, 86, 87, 88, 89, 91, 92, 93, 94, 95, 100, 104, 105, 106, 112, 121, 123, 124, 125, 130, 132, 134, 135, 139, 140, 146, 147, 154, 157, 159, 160, 162, 163, 170, 173, 182, 183, 184, 185, 186, 187, 188, 189, 191, 192, 194, 195

Biblical theology 40

boundary 37, 40, 49, 55, 107, 109, 111, 115, 125, 135, 160

C

Calvin 103, 107, 108, 109, 143, 194

Career 6, 117, 122

Celebrate Recovery 7, 58, 59, 60, 110, 120, 145, 151, 181

Colossians 1:28 171

Colossians 1:9-10 171

Colossians 2:6-7 172

H

Habakkuk 2:5 103, 169
Habakkuk 2:15-16 101, 168
Habakkuk 2:16 102
HCSB 4, 7, 88
heart 11, 12, 16, 17, 19, 20, 22, 30, 31, 46, 54, 59, 66, 70, 86, 93, 94, 95, 96, 98, 104, 120, 121, 133, 144, 158, 160, 165, 173
Hebrews 1:11-14 160
Hebrews 4:12 87, 93
Hebrews 5:11-14 62
Hebrews 5:12-14 172
Hebrews 6:1 172
Holman Christian Standard Bible 7
Homo imbibens 23
Hosea 7:5 102, 169

I

Inaba and Cohen 22, 49, 103, 104
Isaiah 6:3 160
Isaiah 28:1 101, 167
Isaiah 28:7 102, 168
Isaiah 40:8 93
Isaiah 62:8-9 98, 165

J

James 1:23-25 93
Jeremiah 15:16 93
Jeremiah 23:29 93
Jeremiah 31:12 98, 165
Joel 2:24-25 166
John 1:12 161
John 2:7-11 96, 164
John 3:5,
John 3:19 70
John 5:46 93
John 8:34-36 67
John 14:21 70
John 14:23

John 17:3 91
John 17:17 93, 134
Judges 9:13 96, 163

K

Key Events in History Regarding Alcohol 27

L

Lamentations 4:21-22 101, 167
Law of Love 105
Leviticus 23:13 99, 166
Luke 2:52 170
Luke 8:14-15 170
Luke 24:44 93
Luther 103, 107, 108, 109, 194

M

MacArthur, John, 168
Mark 14:25, 76, 144
Marula tree, 3
Matthew 4:4, 73
M11atthew 5:2, 104
Matthew 5:6, 39, 50
Matthew 7:1-5135, 159
Matthew 8:9, 103
Matthew 11:18-19, 76, 144
Matthew 22:17, 50
Matthew 26:26-30, 144
Moderation, 87
Moral Decision-Making Power, 54
motivation in life, 11, 13

N

NA, vii
Narcotics Anonymous, vii, 2, 172
NASB, iv, vii, 42, 68, 69, 76, 77, 78, 81, 82, 137
Natural theology, 20
Nehemiah 8:10, 78, 146

T

U

W

12

—m—

Bibliography

Adams, Jay E. *A Theology of Christian Counseling: More Than Redemption*. Grand Rapids, MI: Zondervan, 1979.

Alcohol Problems and Solutions. "History of Alcohol and Drinking Around the World: Wine, Beer and Spirits (Liquor)." Accessed March 18, 2018. https://www.alcoholproblemsandsolutions.org/history-of-alcohol-and-drinking- around-world/.

Alcoholics Anonymous World Services, Inc. *Twelve Steps and Twelve Traditions*. New York: A.A. Grapevine & Alcoholics Anonymous Publishing, 1981.

Allison, Gregg R. *Historical Theology: An Introduction to Christian Theology*. Grand Rapids, MI: Zondervan, 2011.

Amen, Daniel G. *Change Your Brain, Change Your Life*. New York: Harmony Books, 2015.

—. "Looking at the Brain Changes Everything." Last modified November 1, 2016. Accessed June 15, 20118. www.amenclinics.com

Baker, John. *Celebrate Recovery Leader's Guide*. Grand Rapids, MI: Zondervan, 2012.

Baker, John, Johnny Baker, and Mac Owen. *Celebrate Recovery: 365 Daily Devotionals*. Grand Rapids, MI: Zondervan, 2013.

Baker, Robert A., and John H. Lauders, *A Summary of Christian History*. Nashville, TN: B&H Publishing Group, 2005.

Barnhill, John W., ed. *DSM-5 Clinical Cases*. Washington, DC: American Psychiatric Publishing, 2014.

Beasley-Topliffe, Keith, ed. *The Upper Room Dictionary of Christian Spiritual Formation*. Nashville, TN: Upper Room Books, 2003.

Benner, David G., and Peter C., eds. Hill. *Baker Encyclopedia of Psychology and Counseling*. Grand Rapids, MI: Baker Books, 1999.

Bernard, Harold S. and K. Roy MacKenzie, eds. *Basics of Group Psychotherapy*. New York: The Guilford Press, 1994.

BibleStudy.org. "Wine, Alcohol in Proverbs." Accessed April 4, 2019. http://www.biblestudy.org/bible-study-by-topic/proverbs/alcohol-wine.html

Bloesch, Donald G. *Holy Scripture: Revelation, Inspiration & Interpretation*. Downers Grove, IL: InterVarsity Press, 1994.

Boa, Kenneth, and William Kruidenier, *Romans,* Vol. 6. Nashville, TN: Broadman & Holman Publishers, 2000.

Boice, James Montgomery. *Foundations of the Christian Faith: A Comprehensive and Readable Theology*. Downers Grove, IL: InterVarsity Press, 1986.

Booth, Leo. *Spirituality and Recovery: A Classic Introduction to the Difference Between Spirituality and Religion in the Process of Healing*. Deerfield Beach, FL: Health Communications, Inc., 2012.

Boyce, James P. *Abstract of Systematic Theology*. Low Tide Press: Southern Baptist Theological Seminary, 1887. https://archive.org/stream/abstractofsystem00boyc#page/n5/mode/2up.

Boyer, James L. "A Classification of Imperatives: A Statistical Study," *Grace Theological Journal*, 8, 1987.

Brauch, Manfred T. *Abusing Scripture: The Consequences of Misreading the Bible*. Downers Grove: IL, IVP Academic, 2009.

Brook, David W., and Henry I. Spitz. *The Group Therapy of Substance Abuse.* New York: The Haworth Medical Group, 2002.

Brown, Stephanie, and Virginia Lewis. *The Alcoholic Family in Recovery: A Developmental Model.* New York: The Guilford Press, 1999.

Centers for Disease Control and Prevention (CDC). "Alcohol and Public Health." Accessed June 18, 2018. www.cdc.gov.

Calhoun, Adele Ahlberg. *Spiritual Disciplines Handbook: Practices That Transform Us.* Downers Grove, IL: IVP Books, 2015.

Chafer, Lewis Sperry. *Systematic Theology*, Vol. I. Dallas: Dallas Seminary Press, 1974.

—. *Systematic Theology.* Vol. II. Dallas: Dallas Seminary Press, 1974.

—. *Systematic Theology.* Vol. VIII. Dallas: Dallas Seminary Press, 1974.

Chafer, Lewis Sperry, and John Walvoord. *Major Bible Themes.* Grand Rapids, MI: Zondervan Publishing House, 1974.

Challies, Tim. *The Discipline of Spiritual Discernment.* Wheaton, IL: Crossway, 2007.

Chapell, Bryan. "Grace." In *Systematic Theology Study Bible*. Wheaton, IL: Crossway Books, 2017.

Cheever, Susan. *Drinking in America: Our Secret History.* New York: Grand General Publishing, 2015.

Cheydleur, J. R. "Alcohol-Induced Disorders." In *Baker Encyclopedia of Psychology & Counseling*, David G. Benner and Peter C. Hill, eds. Grand Rapids, MI: Baker Books, 1999.

Clinton, T., and G. Ohlschlager. *Competent Christian Counseling*, Vol 1. Colorado Springs, CO: The Waterbrook Press, 2002.

Clinton, Tim, and Eric Scalise. *Addictions and Recovery Counseling.* Grand Rapids, MI: Baker Books, 2013.

Coombs, R. H., and W. A. Howatt. *The Addiction Counselor's Desk Reference.* Hoboken, NJ: John Wiley & Sons, 2005.

Comfort, Phillip W., and Walter A. Elwell. *Tyndale Bible Dictionary.* Wheaton, IL: Tyndale Publishers, 2001.

Corey, Marianne Schneider, and Gerald Corey. *Groups Process and Practice.* Pacific Grove, CA: Brooks/Cole Publishing Company, 1992.

Daniels, Patricia S. "Your Brain: A User's Guide." *National Geographic: Special Edition.* Washington, D.C.: National Geographic, 2018.

Davis, Ellen F. *Getting Involved with God: Rediscovering the Old Testament.* Chicago: Cowley Publications, 2001.

Diagnostic and Statistical Manual of Mental Disorders, 5th ed. Arlington, VA: American Psychiatric Association. 2013.

Dockery, D. S., ed. "The Pauline Letters." In *Holman Concise Bible Commentary.* Nashville: Broadman & Holman Publishers, 1998.

Dougherty, Ray, and Terry O'Bryan. *Prime for Life: Instructor Manual,* Version 9. Lexington, KY: Prevention Research Institute, 2015.

Drug Free World. "Alcohol: A Short History. Accessed March 18, 2018. https:// www.drugfreeworld.org/drugfacts/alcohol/a-short-history.html.

Earleywine, Mitch. *Substance Use Problems,* 2nd ed. Boston: Hogrefe, 2016. Elwell, W. A, and P. W. Comfort. *Tyndale Bible Dictionary.* Wheaton, IL: Tyndale House Publishers, 2001.

Elwell, Walter A., ed. *The Hendrickson Topical Bible: A Survey of Essential Christian Doctrines.* Peabody, MA: Hendrickson Publishers, 2009.

Emmelkamp, P. M. G., and E. Vedel. *Evidence-Based Treatment for Alcohol and Drug Abuse: A Practitioner's Guide to Theory, Methods, and Practice.* New York: Routledge, 2006.

Ferngren, Gary B., ed. *Science & Religion: A Historical Introduction.* London: John Hopkins University Press, 2002.

Foster, Richard J., and Emilie Griffin, eds. *Spiritual Classics: Selected Readings for Individuals and Groups on the Twelve Spiritual Disciplines.* New York: HarperCollins Publishers, 2000.

Foxe, John. *Foxe's Book of Martyrs.* London: John Day, 1563.

Friends in Recovery. *The Twelve Steps for Christians,* updated ed. Scotts Valley, CA: RPI Publishing, Inc., 2012.

Friesen, Garry. *Decision-Making and the Will of God.* Colorado Springs, CO: Multnomah Books, 2004.

Geisler, Norman L. "A Christian Perspectives on Wine-Drinking." *Bibliotheca Sacra* 139, no. 553 (1982).

—. *Baker Encyclopedia of Christian Apologetics.* Grand Rapids, MI: Baker Books, 1999.

—. *Systematic Theology,* Vol. 1: Introduction; Bible. Minneapolis: Bethany House, 2002.

—. *Systematic Theology,* Vol. 3: Sin and Salvation. Minneapolis: Bethany House, 2004.

Gentry, Kenneth L. *God Gave Wine: What the Bible Says About Alcohol.* Fountain Inn, SC: Victorious Hope Publishing, 2015.

Gil, John. *Gil's Exposition of the Entire Bible.* Bible Hub: Internet Sacred Texts, 2018. Accessed May 27, 2018. http://biblehub.com/commentaries/gill/ genesis/9.htm.

Gilkerson, Luke. "10 Biblical Reasons We Should Appreciate Wine." Accessed June 1, 2018. https://www.intoxicatedonlife.com/authors-lukd-gilkerson.

Gorski, Terence T. *Passages Through Recovery: An Action Plan for Preventing Relapse.* Center City, MN: Hazelden, 1989.

Greggo, Stephen P, and Timothy A. Sisemore, eds. *Counseling and Christianity: Five Approaches.* Downers Grove, IL: IVP Academic, 2012.

Griffiths, C. A. "The Theories, Mechanisms, Benefits, and Practical Delivery of Psychosocial Educational Interventions for People with Mental Health Disorders." *International Journal of Psychosocial Rehabilitation,* 11(1) (2006).

Gough, L. F. "A Study of Luke 14:26: Jesus Calls His Disciples to a Life of Supreme Commitment." *Ashland Theological Journal,* Volume 3, 3 (1970).

Grudem, Wayne. *Systematic Theology: An Introduction to Biblical Doctrine.* Grand Rapids, MI: Zondervan, 2000.

Hanson, David J. *Preventing Alcohol Abuse: Alcohol, Culture and Control.* Praeger, 1995.

Hauerwas, Stanley. "Salvation and Health: Why Medicine Needs the Church." In *On Moral Medicine: Theological Perspectives in Medical Ethics,* 2nd ed., Stephen E. Lammers and Allen Verhey, eds. Grand Rapids, MI: William B. Eerdmans Publishing Company, 1998.

Hemfelt, Robert, Richard Fowler, Frank Minirth, and Paul Meier. *The Path to Serenity: The Book of Spiritual Growth and Personal Change Through Twelve- Step Recovery.* Nashville: Thomas Nelson Publishers, 1991.

Henry, Matthew. *Matthew Henry's Bible Commentary.* Christianity. com. Accessed May 28, 2018. https://www.christianity.com/bible/ commentary. php?com=mhc&b=19&c=19

Horton, Michael. *We Believe: Recovering the Essentials of the Apostles' Creed.* Waco, TX: Word Publishing, 1998.

Hunt, June. *Counseling Through Your Bible Handbook: Providing Biblical Hope and Practical Help for 50 Everyday Problems.* Eugene, OR: Harvest House, 2008.

Inaba, D S, and W E Cohen. *Uppers, Downers, All-Arounders: Physical and Mental Effects of Psychoactive Drugs,* 8th ed. Medford, OR: CNS Productions, Inc, 2014.

International Bible Society. *The Journey of Recovery: New Testament.* Colorado Springs, CO: International Bible Society, n.d.

Jaeggli, Randy. *Christians and Alcohol: A Scriptural Case for Abstinence.* Greenville, SC: BJU Press, 2014.

Jarvis, Tracey J., Jenny Tebbutt, Richard P. Marrick, and Fiona Shand, eds. *Treatment Approaches for Alcohol and Drug Dependence: An Introductory Guide,* 2nd ed. Chichester, England: John Wiley & Sons, 2005.

Jellinek, E. M. *The Disease Concept of Alcoholism.* Mansfield Centre, CT: Martino Publishing, 2010.

Jennings, Timothy R. *The God-Shaped Brain: How Changing Your View of God Transforms Your Life.* Downers Grove, IL: IVP Books, 2017.

Jeremiah, David. *Understanding the Books of the Bible.* San Diego, CA: Turning Point, 2014.

Johnson, Eric L. *God and Soul Care.* Downers Grove, IL: IVP Books, 2017. Jones, David W. *Knowing and Doing the Will of God.* Wake Forest, NC: Veritas Publications, 2017.

Kirwan, William T. *Biblical Concepts for Christian Counseling: A Case for Integrating Psychology and Theology.* Grand Rapids, MI: Baker Academic, 1984.

Kittel, G. W. Bromiley, and G. Friedrich, eds. *Theological Dictionary of the New Testament,* Vol. 1 (Grand Rapids, MI: Eerdmans, electronic ed.).

Kruse, C. G. *John: An Introduction and Commentary,* Vol. 4 (Downers Grove, IL: InterVarsity Press, 2003), 232.

Kuhn, Cynthia, Scott Swartzwelder, and Wilkie Wilson. *Buzzed: The Straight Facts About the Most Used and Abused Drugs,* 3rd ed. New York: W. W. Norton & Company, 2008.

Laidlaw, John "The Immaterial Part of Man." In *Systematic Theology, Vol. II,* Lewis Sperry Chafer, 191-192 (Dallas: Dallas Seminary Press, 1974).

Lambert, Heath. *A Theology of Biblical Counseling: The Doctrinal Foundations of Counseling Ministry*. Grand Rapids, MI: Zondervan, 2016.

Larson, K. *I & II Thessalonians, I & II Timothy, Titus, Philemon* Vol. 9. Nashville, TN: Broadman & Holman Publishers, 2000.

La Salvia, T.A. "Enhancing Addiction Treatment Through Psychoeducational Groups," *Journal of Substance Abuse Treatment.* September-October, Vol. 10 (1993).

Lewis, C. S. *The Complete C. S. Lewis Signature Classics.* San Francisco: HarperSanFrancisco, 2002.

Lewis, Marc. *The Biology of Desire: Why Addiction Is Not a Disease.* New York: PublicAffairs, 2016.

Litchfield, Bruce, and Nellie Litchfield. *Christian Counseling and Family Therapy,* 2nd ed. Canberra, Australia: Litchfield Family Services, 2006.

Louw, J. P., and E. A. Nida. *Greek-English Lexicon of the New Testament: Based on Semantic Domains*, Vol. 1. New York: United Bible Societies, 1996.

Loyola Marymount University. "History of Alcohol Use." Accessed March 18, 2018. https://www.academics.imu.edu/headsup/forstudents/historyofacoholuse/.

Lumpkins, Peter. *Alcohol Today: Abstinence in an Age of Indulgence.* Garland, Texas: Hannibal Books, 2009. MacArthur, John. *Faith Works.* London: Word Publishing, 1993.

—. *The Gospel According to Jesus.* Grand Rapids, MI: Zondervan Publishing House, 1994.

—. *The MacArthur Study Bible.* Nashville: Word Publishing, 1997.

—. *Right Thinking in a World Gone Wrong: A Biblical Response to Today's Most Controversial Issues.* Eugene, OR: Harvest House Publishers, 2009.

—. *Found: God's Will.* Colorado Springs, CO: David C. Cook, 2012.

—. *The MacArthur Bible Handbook: A Book-by-Book Exploration of God's Word.* Nashville: Thomas Nelson Inc, 2013.

—. *The Gospel According to God.* Wheaton, IL: Crossway Books, 2018.
Malcomson, Keith. *Sober Saints.* n.c.: Keith Malcomson, 2013.

Masters, Peter. *Should Christians Drink? The Biblical Case for Abstinence.* Swansea, UK: Harcourt Colourprint, 2017.

May, Gerald G. *Addiction and Grace: Love and Spirituality in the Healing of Addictions.* New York: HarperOne, 1988.

McDonald, James, ed. *Christ-Centered Biblical Counseling.* Eugene, OR: Harvest House Publishers, 2013.

McDowell, Josh. *A Ready Defense.* San Bernadino, CA: Here's Life Publishers, 1992.

McGrath, Alister E., and James I. Packer, eds. *Zondervan Handbook of Christian Beliefs.* Grand Rapids, MI: The Zondervan Corporation, 2005.

McMinn, Mark R., and Clark D. Campbell. *Integrative Psychotherapy: A Comprehensive Christian Approach.* Downers Grove, IL: IVP Academic, 2007.

Mee-Lee, D, G. D. Shulman, M. Fishman, D. R. Gastfriend, J. H. Griffith, eds. *ASAM Patient Placement Criteria for the Treatment of Substance-Related Disorders.* Chevy Chase, MD: American Society of Addiction Medicine, Inc., 2001.

Meier, Paul D, Frank B. Minirth, Frank B. Wichern, and Donald E. Ratcliff. *Introduction to Psychology and Counseling: Christian Perspectives and Applications,* 2nd ed. Grand Rapids: Baker Books, 1991.

Melick, R. R. *Philippians, Colossians, Philemon,* Vol. 32. Nashville: Broadman & Holman Publishers, 1991.

Millon, Theodore, Paul H. Blaney, and Rodger D. Davis. *The Oxford Textbook of Psychopathology*. New York: Oxford University Press, 1999.

Minirth, Frank, Paul Meier, Siegfried Fink, Walter Byrd, and Don Hawkins. *Taking Control*. Grand Rapids, MI: Baker Book House, 1988.

Morris, Leon. *Luke: An Introduction and Commentary*, Vol. 3. Downers Grove, IL: InterVarsity Press, 1988.

Mounce, Robert H. *Romans*, Vol. 27. Nashville: Broadman & Holman Publishers, 1995.

Narcotics Anonymous. "Alcohol History." Accessed March 18, 2018. https://www.narconon.org/drug-information/alcohol-history.html.

—. *Just for Today: Daily Meditations for Recovering Addicts*. Van Nuys, CA: Narcotics Anonymous World Services, Inc., 1992.

National Geographic Magazine. "Our 9,000-Year Love Affair with Booze." Accessed March 18, 2018. https://www.nationalgeographic.com/magazine/2017/02/alcohol-discovery-   addiction-booze-human-culture/.

—. "Your Brain: 100 Things You Never Knew." Washington, D.C.: *National Geographic*, 2018.

National Institute on Alcohol Abuse and Alcoholism. "Alcoholism: Natural History and Background." Accessed March 18, 2018. https://www.niaaa.nih.gov/problems/healthdisparities;alcoholism1.htm.

—. "Drinking Levels Defined." Accessed June 18, 2018. https://www.niaaa.nih.gov/problems/drinking_levels_defined.

National Institute on Drug Abuse, "Drug Abuse and Addiction" in *Drugs, Brains, and Behavior: The Science of Addiction*, July 2014. Accessed 6 July 2018. https://www.drugabuse.gov/publications/drugs-brains-behavior-science- addiction/drug-abuse-addiction.

Nichols, Stephen J. *Pages from Church History*. Phillipsburg, NJ: P&R Publishing, 2006.

—. "Humanity." In the *Systematic Theology Study Bible*. Wheaton, IL: Crossway Books, 2017.

O'Brien, Kevin S. J. *The Ignatian Adventure*. Chicago: Loyola Press, 2011.

"Odysseus, Precommitment, and the Siren Song." In Hack the System. Last modified October 2, 2012. Accessed June 2, 2019. http://hackthesystem. com/ blog/odysseus-precommitment-and-the-siren-song/.

Pickover, Clifford A. *The Physics Book*. New York: Barnes & Noble, 2011. Porter, William. *Alcohol Explained*. n.c.: William Porter, n.d.

Quora, accessed April 24, 2019. https://www.quora.com/ How-much-do-Americans-spend-on-booze-each-year

Rana, Fazale. *The Cell's Design: How Chemistry Reveals the Creator's Artistry*. Grand Rapids, MI: Baker Books, 2008.

Raymond, I. W. *The Teaching of the Early Church on the Use of Wine and Strong Drink*. AMS Press, 1927.

Richards, P. Scott, and Allen E. Bergin. *A Spiritual Strategy for Counseling and Psychotherapy*. Washington, D.C.: American Psychological Association, 1997.

Robertson, Archibald T. *Word Pictures in the New Testament*. Grand Rapids, MI: Zondervan Publishing House, 1933.

Rutzky, Jacques. *Coyote Speaks: Creative Strategies for Psychotherapists Treating Alcoholics and Addicts*. London: Jason Aronson, Inc., 1998).

Ryrie, Charles C. *The Ryrie Study Bible*. Chicago: Moody Press, 1978.

—. *Basic Theology: A Popular Systematic Guide to Understanding Biblical Truth*. Chicago: Moody Press, 1999.

Scazzero, Peter. *Emotionally Healthy Spirituality*. Grand Rapids, MI: Zondervan, 2006.

Substance Abuse and Mental Health Services Administration (SAMHSA). "Substance Use Disorders." Last modified October 27, 2015, accessed June 15, 2018. www.SAMHSA.gov.

Schaff, Philip. *History of the Christian Church*, Vol. 7. Peabody, MA: Hendrickson Publishers Marketing LLC, 2011.

Shapiro, Rami. *Recovery-The Sacred Art: The Twelve Steps as Spiritual Practice.* Woodstock, VT: Skylight Paths, 2013.

Shaw, Mark E. *Divine Intervention: Hope and Help for Families of Addicts.* Bemidji, MN: Focus Publishing, 2011.

—. *Relapse Biblical Prevention Strategies.* Focus Publishing, Inc: www. histruthin- love.org, 2011.

—. *The Heart of Addiction: A Biblical Perspective.* Bemidji, MN: Focus Publishing, Inc, 2008.

Skrant, Larry. *Addicts at the Cross: A Christian's 9-Step Program Big Book.* Abbotsford, WI: Aneko Press, 2016.

Stanford, Matthew S. *Grace for the Afflicted.* Downers Grove, IL: IVP Books, 2017.

Smith, David E., and Richard B. Seymour. *Clinician's Guide to Substance Abuse.* New York: McGraw-Hill Medical Publishing Division, 2001.

Stanford, Matthew S. *Grace for the Afflicted: A Clinical and Biblical Perspective on Mental Illness.* Downers Grove: IL: InterVarsity Press, 2017.

Sterns, Richard. *Unfinished: Believing Is Only the Beginning.* Nashville: Thomas Nelson, 2013.

Stott, John. *Basic Christianity.* Downers Grove, IL: InterVaristy Press, 1971. Swain, Scott R. "Revelation." In *Systematic Theology Study Bible.* Wheaton, IL: Crossway Books, 2017.

Tan, Siang-Yang. *Counseling and Psychotherapy: A Christian Perspective.* Grand Rapids, MI: Baker Books, 2011.

Thomas, W. H. Griffith. "The Principles of Theology: Introduction to the Thirty- Nine Articles." Accessed May 31, 2018. http://www. preachershelp.net/wp-content/uploads/2014/11/griffith-thomas-39-articles.pdf

Thompson, Curt. *Anatomy of the Soul.* Carol Stream, IL: Tyndale, 2010.

Trimpey, Jack. "Rational Recovery," accessed June 15, 2018. https://www. the-alcoholism-guide.org/rational-recovery.html.

Truth by Grace. "How Has the Church Historically Viewed Alcohol?" Accessed March 18, 2018. https://www.truthbygrace.org/ how-has-the-church-historically-viewed-alcohol/.

Vallant, George E. *The Natural History of Alcoholism, Revisited.* London: Harvard Univrsity Press, 1995.

Velasquez, Mary Warden, Cathy Crouch, Nanette Stokes Stephens, and Carlo C. DiClemente. *Group Treatment for Substance Abuse: A Stages of Change Therapy Manual*, 2nd ed. New York: The Guilford Press, 2016.

Von Buseck, Craig. "What Are the Three Parts of Man?" accessed on May 27, 2018. http://www1.cbn.com/questions/what-are-the-three-parts-of-man

Wag. "Strabismus," accessed on December 27, 2018. https://wagwalking. com/ condition/strabismus.

Wallace, Daniel B. *Greek Grammar Beyond the Basics: An Exegetical Syntax of the New Testament.* Grand Rapids, MI: Zondervan Publishing House, 1996.

Waltke, Bruce K. *Finding the Will of God: A Pagan Notion?* Gresham, OR: Vision House Publishing Inc., 1995.

—. *The Book of Proverbs: Chapters 15-31.* Grand Rapids, MI: William B. Eerdmans Publishing Company, 2005.

Warren, Rick. *The Purpose Driven Life.* Grand Rapids, MI: Zondervan, 2002.

Welch, Edward T. *Addictions: A Banquet in the Grave; Finding Hope in the Power of the Gospel.* Phillipsburg, NJ: P&R Publishing Company, 2001.

Wells, David. "What Is Doctrine and Why Is It Important?" In *Systematic Theology Study Bible.* Wheaton, IL: Crossway, 2017.

West, Jim. *Drinking with Calvin and Luther: A History of Alcohol in the Church.* Oakdown: Lincoln, CA, 2003.

White, Sadie Ann. "Human Person" in *The Oxford Companion to the Bible.* Bruce M. Metzger, and Michael D. Coogan, eds. New York: Oxford University Press, 1993.

Whittington, Brad. *What Would Jesus Drink? What the Bible Really Says About Alcohol.* Austin, TX: WP Press, 2011.

Wiersbe, Warren W. *Be Commited.* Wheaton, IL: Victor Books, 1993.

Wilkerson, David R. *Sipping Saints: Do Christianity and Drinking Mix?* Old Tappan, NJ: Fleming H. Revell Company, 1978.

Witmer, John A. "Romans." In J. F. Walvoord, and R. B. Zuck, eds. *The Bible Knowledge Commentary: An Exposition of the Scriptures,* Vol. 2. Wheaton, IL: Victor Books, 1985.

Worthington, E. L., J. L. Hunter, C. B. Sharp, J. N. Hook, D. R. Van Tongeren, and D. E. Monforte-Milton. "A Psychoeducational Intervention to Promote Forgiveness in Christians in the Philippines." *Journal of Mental Health Counseling 32* (1), 2010.

Yalom, I. D. *The Theory and Practice of Group Psychotherapy,* 5th ed. New York: Basic Books, 2005.

Young, Frances. *Brokenness and Blessing: Toward a Biblical Spirituality.* Grand Rapids, MI: Baker Academic.

Young, Robert. *Analytical Concordance to the Bible.* Grand Rapids, MI: Eerdmans Publishing Company, 1975.

Zielinski, Sarah. "The Alcoholics of the Animal World." Smithsonian.com. Accessed May 27, 2018. https://www.smithsonianmag.com/science-nature/ the-alcoholics-of-the-animal-world-81007700/